JERKS
AT
WORK

D0995423

30131 05780014 3

LONDON BOROUGH OF BARNET

JERKS AT WORK

Toxic Coworkers and
What to Do About Them

TESSA WEST

1

Ebury Edge, an imprint of Ebury Publishing,
20 Vauxhall Bridge Road,
London SW1V 2SA

Ebury Edge is part of the Penguin Random House group of companies
whose addresses can be found at global.penguinrandomhouse.com

Copyright © Tessa West 2022

Tessa West has asserted her right to be identified as the author of this
Work in accordance with the Copyright, Designs and Patents Act 1988

First published in the United States by Portfolio in 2022
First published in the United Kingdom by Ebury Edge in 2022

Some names and identifying characteristics of people whose stories may be
included in this book have been changed to protect their privacy.

Book design by Chris Welch

www.penguin.co.uk

A CIP catalogue record for this book is available from the British Library

ISBN 9781529146035

Printed and bound in Great Britain by Clays Ltd, Elcograf S.p.A.

The authorised representative in the EEA is Penguin Random House Ireland,
Morrison Chambers, 32 Nassau Street, Dublin D02 YH68

Penguin Random House is committed to a sustainable future for
our business, our readers and our planet. This book is made
from Forest Stewardship Council® certified paper.

FOR MY FAMILY—JAY, MATTY, JACK,

ANNIE, MY PARENTS, AND MY BROTHER,

JUSTIN—WHO GAVE ME INSPIRATION FOR

MY STORIES, AND FOR MY STUDENTS AND

LONGTIME COLLABORATORS, WHO'VE

SHOWN ME HOW AMAZING WORK CAN

BE WHEN YOU DO IT ALONGSIDE THE

RIGHT PEOPLE. NOT A DAY GOES BY

I DON'T THINK TO MYSELF,

DAMN, I'M LUCKY TO BE HERE.

CONTENTS

INTRODUCTION

"If I don't double my sales by the end of the month, Sasha will skewer me. She just gave this *horrible* speech to my team about how I am such a disappointment."

Annie sat slumped over her happy hour cocktail, catching up her former colleague Calvin about what had gone down over the past two months. Shortly after she was hired, Annie's boss, David, hastily left the New York office to deal with a supply chain problem in Asia. With little time to find a replacement, he put Sasha at the helm.

Sasha wasn't particularly talented at any one thing but perfectly adequate at a number of things. She had spent ten years in the New York office and had a wealth of institutional knowledge. Not very many people could tell you who in sales is the most socially suited for dinner with clients *and* how to fix the broken video projector.

But above all else, she was clever with money. Sasha was a real detail sleuth, spending hours poring over budget sheets to cut a dollar here, a dollar there. People griped about her cuts ("Where did the espresso machine go?"), but David didn't care. He liked saving money. And with every additional month he stayed in Asia, Sasha sank her claws deeper into the company—first taking over all small-scale budget decisions, then inching her way into hiring and promotion. Once she started controlling the sales team, all hell broke loose.

Sasha was the Frankenstein's monster of bosses at work—undercutting people in front of their teams, micromanaging them, and changing direction so many times it made people's heads spin. In meetings, she had an unpredictability that left everyone on edge, all smiles and compliments one moment, torturous acts of humiliation the next. She also wore so much perfume it left Annie with a low-grade headache anytime she spent more than ten minutes in a room with her.

In the early days while David was still closely monitoring her, Sasha was charming, almost obsequious. She sent Annie emails that said things like, "I'm so honored to be working with you, and I hope some of your magic rubs off on me. Can we set up some weekly training sessions?" The emails stopped once David no longer insisted that she cc him on everything.

In fact, once David checked out entirely, Sasha's true, terrible colors began to show.

Like a lot of jerks at work, Sasha started with small, public acts of criticism meant to damage Annie's reputation. Each week, Annie would hold a meeting with her sales team. About a month into the job, she noticed Sasha sneaking in during the last five minutes.

"Hi Annie! Do you mind if I chat with your team for a few minutes?" she asked sheepishly.

Once Annie was out of earshot, Sasha would question Annie's

decisions ("Are you sure that's a good idea?") and undercut her expertise in front of her direct reports ("I know that client well—much better than Annie; he will never go for it"). Then she would spread weird and wrong gossip about her, which Annie figured was an attempt to build rapport with the team.

The micromanagement started off with small, arbitrary changes to Annie's budgets. Daily food allowances requested at forty-five dollars a day were changed to forty dollars, for no other reason than to remind Annie who was really in charge. Sometimes Sasha would increase Annie's budgets, which made no sense at all.

Over time, Sasha oscillated between jealous and downright patronizing, sometimes within an hour. When Annie tried to make autonomous decisions, Sasha assured her that "David wants me to oversee *everything* and *everyone*." Small changes to her budgets became massive overhauls. It became impossible for Annie to execute a sales contract without Sasha getting in the way.

Then came the firing.

Sasha was having a tough time containing gossip about herself and she was becoming paranoid. Like a dictator losing her grasp on her people, she started cutting off heads left and right. Sometimes she would bring in groups of people to her office and fire all of them at once; it was quicker that way. Annie assured her team that she could protect them, but she wasn't so certain. The anxiety was so staggering, it overshadowed everyone's progress. They stopped celebrating wins. They stopped having lunches out together. Everyone was happy if they just made it through another day.

Most people, including Calvin, jumped ship as soon as things went south; they weren't going to sit around and watch their workplace turn into a hellscape. Annie, on the other hand, had remained and tried to stay positive. But it was getting harder every day.

During this period, Annie made several attempts to contact David. Things were not going well in Asia, and most of her emails were met with autoreplies. Eventually she landed a video call with him at two a.m. her time. But before the words were out of her mouth—"Sasha is a terror and she's destroying this company"— she knew her approach wouldn't work. David looked exhausted, like a man who had walked this road several times before and had yet to find a detour.

"Listen. I know Sasha can be tough, but she is doing a lot. The best I can do is decrease the amount of face time you have to spend with her," he told Annie. He ended the call with some words of encouragement and begged her to "just stick it out until this supply problem gets resolved."

Most of you are probably thinking at this point in the story, "What is wrong with you, Annie? Why don't you get the hell out?" It seems obvious in hindsight that Annie should have left as soon as David handed over the reins to Sasha, like Calvin did. But for Annie, giving up her dream job was unthinkable. Even at the worst of times, David kept dangling a carrot in front of her: "Remember, Sasha is temporary." Denial can lead us to make all sorts of bad decisions in life, including career ones. Besides, like many of us, Annie didn't want a short-lived stint; she wanted to settle down and make a home for herself at this company. And when she interviewed for the job, she'd been assured she would have the opportunity to do so. "We want to build you up, not train you and lose you." Ever heard that one before?

Annie had believed it. Why wouldn't she? But now she had a series of ailments more common among people in their eighties than people in their thirties. In the last year, her blood pressure spiked, her sleep dropped from eight to five hours a night, and her clean, green diet slowly gave way to hot dogs and beer. Her hair was thinning. She had a weird eye twitch. Her limbs started tingling the minute she lay down. She probably had a drinking problem too, but she wasn't ready to admit it.

As the bartender approached, Annie looked down at her maraschino cherry. Dark, dank, and cheap, this bar was the local watering hole for all hard-done-by employees within a five-block radius too depressed to chat it up. Which now included her.

"Annie, let me be frank," said Calvin. "You look more like a prison guard who broke up a fight at the end of her shift than vice president of sales for a high-end leisurewear brand. I can see where this is going, and it isn't good."

Calvin was six months post-Sasha and looked fresh-faced and fit as a fiddle—he didn't belong in this bar. Now working for a competitor, he spent his afternoons sipping lattes and sharing yoga tips with his boss. He had an air of superiority about him that reminded Annie of those people in college who finished finals early and would play volleyball in front of the library, taunting the studiers inside. "It sucks to be you," their cocky little faces said.

But he was right.

"Don't you understand?" Calvin said, "You could put a gun to David's head, and he wouldn't be able to tell you who works here and how much money the company grossed last year. No one knows the details of this company like Sasha knows them. David can't fire her even if he wanted to; he's completely dependent on her. Sasha is here to stay."

Most of us have worked with someone who had an outsized effect on our emotional well-being. To cope, we've tried a few tactics: venting to friends, disengaging from the social scene at work, gossiping about the person in the hopes that our bosses will learn—via the grapevine—just how miserable we are.

The boldest among us try direct confrontation. But these interactions often end in more conflict, since most people don't enjoy having their flaws spelled out to them in excruciating detail. When confrontations fail, we often go to the next person in charge and beg for help. But even the most sympathetic bosses are often ill-equipped to handle problem people at work. Some—like David—are too dependent on your jerk to act against them. Others agree there's a problem, but they feel helpless to stop it. Yet others are so averse to confrontation, the very thought of standing up to a jerk at work makes them weak in the knees.

When direct feedback fails, we tend to turn to all-out avoidance. I once rearranged my work hours to avoid sharing a bathroom with a jerk at work. It was inconvenient and bad for my sleep, but at least I got about six stress-free hours a day to myself.

And I don't think I'm alone.

Thankfully, it doesn't have to be this way. You no longer have to be beholden to soul-sucking jerks at work and the chaos they inflict on your life. By learning what motivates them to do what they do, and by applying the research-based strategies found in this book, you can equip yourself to handle those who deplete your energy and cost you emotional well-being and—finally—take back your peace of mind.

As a social psychologist, I've studied how people communicate for nearly two decades. I've observed the strategies we use to negotiate, collaborate, argue effectively, and successfully avoid one another. I've measured the stress people feel when interactions go poorly, how that stress manifests in the body, and how quickly stress can spread from one person to another.

I've also seen what happens when relationship problems at work go unresolved and leak into every aspect of our lives—from how we interact with our kids to how connected we feel to our romantic partners. And by leveraging social science, I've helped people, from new employees to C-suite executives, solve their jerk-at-work problems.

HOW YOU SHOULD READ THIS BOOK

Getting a handle on your jerk at work is little like profiling a serial killer. In other words, you first need to get into your jerk's head to learn what makes them tick. How do they pick their victims? How have they avoided capture? Do they have a boss who (secretly) benefits from their behavior?

To help you on your profiling journey, I've created a taxonomy of jerks at work.

Jerks at Work
Kiss Up/Kick Downers
Credit Stealers
Bulldozers
Free Riders
Micromanagers
Neglectful Bosses
Gaslighters

Kiss up/kick downers have a singular goal in mind: to climb to the top by any means necessary. To get there, they treat everyone who is at the same level or below them as competition. They reserve their good manners for the people in charge.

Credit stealers are wolves in sheep's clothing—they are our teammates and mentors who look out only for themselves. Credit stealers seem like friends, but they will betray your trust if your idea is good enough to steal. They help with a project but undermine your contributions when presenting it to the boss. They help you work through half-baked ideas only to take credit for them later. They are the leaders who offer to help you thrive but are secretly jealous of your success. They tend to be good at covering their tracks.

Bulldozers are seasoned, well-connected employees who aren't afraid to flex their muscles to get what they want. They have two trademark moves: they take over the process of group decision-making, and they render bosses powerless to stop them through fear and intimidation. Most know how to go over the boss's head to get what they want—they know who, at a level or two above them, will take them seriously. Truth be told, a lot of workplaces value this type of "leadership behavior"—the squeaky wheel gets the grease. But for those of us stuck working with a bulldozer, decisions often grind to a halt until this person gets their way. These jerks have no interest in compromising.

Free riders are experts at doing nothing and getting rewarded for it. They often take on work that has the veneer of importance but requires very little effort. They thrive in well-functioning teams, such as those with conscientious people who pick up their slack and those with a strong sense of cohesion. Most of them are well-liked and friendly, making them difficult to call out.

Micromanagers are impatient taskmasters who disrespect your personal space and time. Some do it because they used to have your job and they're having a hard time moving on, others because they're under the false impression that more monitoring equals better performance. Micromanagement isn't a scalable strategy, so micromanaging bosses often put people in rotation. When you're out of rotation, don't expect to hear from your boss for days, sometimes weeks on end. Micromanagers also tend to be neglectful bosses.

Neglectful bosses hate being out of the loop. But for lots of reasons (micromanaging is one), they often are. Most follow a three-step process: long periods of neglect, a buildup of anxiety from not having a handle on things, and finally a surge of control over you to alleviate their anxiety. If you have a neglectful boss, you live in a world of chronic uncertainty, making these jerks at work one of the most difficult to handle.

Gaslighters lie with the intent of deceiving on a grand scale. They isolate their victims first, then slowly build an alternative reality that suits their needs. Some gaslighters isolate by making victims feel like their position at work is precarious, others by making their victims feel special, like they are part of a secret club. Gaslighting is often a means to an end; it allows coworkers and bosses to get away with things such as cheating and stealing that they could not do alone.

Each chapter in this book is dedicated to a different jerk at work. First, you'll learn the hallmark characteristics of each type, what drives their behavior, and how it is most likely to show up. Second, I lay out time-proven strategies, tips, and tricks for handling each jerk. The solutions here don't require you to be a mind-reading expert. Anyone can use the tactics I cover, including those who prefer to avoid conflict.

The chapters are written independently, so you can reference each type as they become relevant. I do, however, cross-reference the types occasionally, so reading the chapters in order will help you see the similarities and differences between them. You will also see how the same strategies can work for multiple types of jerks.

This book is meant to be a guide you can return to anytime a new jerk-at-work problem crops up. People who are new at work will read it with a different set of eyes than those who have been on the job for years. And as you gain experience and switch jobs, you can go back to it and get insights you missed the first time around. Similarly, it's recommended that you flip to the back and take the quizzes there twice: right now before you read the rest of this book, and again after—you might see a change.

THE TRUTH ABOUT JERKS AT WORK

Throughout my career, I've heard a lot of misconceptions about jerks at work. Clearing these up is the first step in solving a jerk-at-work problem.

MISCONCEPTION 1: ONLY INEXPERIENCED PEOPLE STRUGGLE WITH JERKS AT WORK

Lots of people have come to me, with years of workplace experience under their belts, embarrassed that after all this time they still don't have a handle on their relationship problems at work. I remind them not to confuse time spent on something with progress.

No matter how educated you are or what your job title is, you can fall victim to a jerk at work. Spending time in the workplace does not necessarily translate to having better conflict management skills.

Most of us never formally learn these skills. Management courses and leadership training focus largely on the types of behaviors you should be engaging in (and those that you should avoid), but they rarely focus on how to use your social network to solve workplace problems or how to frame problems in ways that will get higher-status people to care. These skills require knowledge of how relationships function at work.

It is never too early, or too late, to learn the tactics I cover in this book.

MISCONCEPTION 2: JERKS AT WORK ARE BITTER EMPLOYEES WITH NO REAL SKILLS

"The only reason why Bob is torturing me is because he's jealous and doesn't know any other way of getting ahead."

I hear comments like this a lot. It's easy to villainize jerks at work—to assume that they are talentless asshats who have nothing better to do with their time than make our lives miserable. But I don't think this approach gets us very far. Every workplace has at least one person who is willing to use their talent in nefarious ways. The trick is figuring out what those talents are.

Most jerks are skilled social perceivers with lots of social connections; underestimating them won't get you anywhere. This book will help you figure out what those talents are so you can learn how to outwit these people.

MISCONCEPTION 3: MY BOSSES AREN'T DOING ANYTHING ABOUT MY JERK BECAUSE THEY DON'T CARE

The sad reality is, most people aren't promoted into leadership positions because they know how to manage people; they're promoted because they were good at their old job. A lot of jerk-at-work problems can be traced back to poor leadership. Even well-intentioned bosses often don't know how to handle office jerks.

Sometimes the problem boils down to time, resources, and priorities. Bosses with too much on their plates drop the ball on communicating with their employees. They assume that no news is good news, and one-on-one conversations are reserved for putting out fires. Efficient employees with good track records receive the least attention, as do the people in highly efficient teams. Jerks like the free rider flourish with bosses like these—they know their teammates won't complain about them, they'll just compensate for their laziness.

Other bosses inadvertently trust jerks at work to do the communicating for them. The kiss up/kick downer, for example, is a master at making themselves trustworthy. Through a series of small, manipulative steps, they manage to become the liaison between the boss and other employees. Bosses like Sasha, holding down the fort while the real boss is out of town, can get away with almost anything because no one is monitoring them.

It's easy to blame our jerk-at-work problems on our bosses. In this book, I teach you how to move beyond the blame to think about why your boss is contributing to the problem. Some leaders are trying to fit into a world with bad workplace norms, have bosses who are horrible mentors themselves, or aren't stellar communicators and don't know how to get better. You will learn how to understand why your boss behaves the way they do and what might be keeping them from taking your side.

My hope is that as you learn strategies for dealing with difficult people, you will see an increase in your own psychological feelings of certainty. Most of us can handle problems at work if we can predict them and then strategize what to do. Expect to feel more empowered and less anxious. Gone will be the days where you tiptoe around your jerk, coming to the office only when they're gone, or climbing the stairs to avoid seeing them in the elevator.

After years studying how people communicate with one another, the single most important lesson I've learned is this: we will never solve our jerk-at-work problems until we understand how to leverage our social relationships.

In other words, the antidote to jerks at work is friends at work. My goal for you is not to wind up like Annie—admitting to yourself that your job is just a stepping-stone, that you have only two choices: grin and bear it or get the hell out. My goal is to teach you how enlist the help of others to get what you want.

Sometimes the people who are the most helpful aren't on your radar yet—they work at arm's length from you but are well positioned within your social network to connect you to people in power. In fact, arms-length coworkers are often better allies than close friends. In this book, I recommend that you develop relationships that are wide (with lots of people in your professional social network) and not just deep (with a handful of people with whom you feel close).

If you're socially isolated or new at work and don't have a lot of relationships, I will teach you how to make them. A surprising 70 percent of people say that having friends at work is the most crucial element to a happy working life. But when it comes to dealing with jerks, we often try to go it alone.

If you feel yourself uncomfortably identifying more with the jerk than the victim, that's okay too. Relating to the jerks is one of the more unexpected experiences of reading this book. We all have a jerk lurking deep inside of us. It's part of human nature. In fact, the day I decided to write this book was the day that I realized I had become the evil protagonist in my own jerk-at-work story.

Through a series of unfortunate events, I wound up on the subway on my way to a kid's birthday party in Queens, New York, drinking rosé out of a can. I bought the can (and three more just like it) because it could have passed for fancy sparkling water.

The week before was rough.

One of my jobs at work was to implement a big office move. For the first time in decades, our space was getting renovated—new paint colors and lots of light—and we had only to move down the hall and up a flight of stairs.

My coworker Jon and I had spent several months going back and forth about the plan, and we finally were ready to present it to the group. About half of my coworkers showed up to the meeting in person, and the remaining eight or so video-conferenced in, their faces awkwardly squished on the screen (this was pre-pandemic, before we got the hang of it).

We knew that people were feeling apprehensive, so we came prepared with a long list of all the ways in which our coworkers' lives would be made better, not worse, by the move. More square footage. Better lighting. You know that weird black soot that comes down from the ceiling and makes a neat pile on your desk every day? Gone.

No one cared about the list.

Instead, most people were flat-out confused about why we were doing the move in the first place, some because they had been minimally engaged with the move all along, others because the plans had changed so many times it was impossible to remember why exactly we weren't allowed to do things such as move walls. But confusion was quickly replaced by fear, and in some cases anger. "Why are we doing this at all? I *like* the old space!" one person yelled into the abyss, their video on accidental mute.

I immediately became prickly and defensive. This was the plan and we were sticking to it; I didn't care how anyone felt about it. I left the meeting in a huff, full of irritation that my work was underappreciated.

It took some time (and a few of those rosé cans), but upon reflection, it was clear that over months of planning and prepping, I had become an accidental bulldozer. I hadn't intended on shutting people down or telling them that their feelings didn't matter, but I did.

Achieving my goal had given me tunnel vision. I had failed to take my own advice and see the move through my coworkers' perspectives—what it must feel like to be told that you need to leave your workspace after ten, sometimes twenty, years.

I had also made people feel uncertain about their future at work—unsure of what their day-to-day would look like and whether they would run into their own nemeses in the bathroom. For people dealing with jerks at work, feelings of uncertainty and a lack of control over their own outcomes are common psychological experiences.

The good news is, jerks at work can change their ways, and I was able to repair my relationships using a handful of tactics I cover in this book. Bulldozers stifle the voices of others, so I gave people the chance to be heard—asking them for their perspectives and getting to the bottom of their biggest concerns. We created rules that allowed everyone to weigh in on important decisions, so that no one person (me) was making decisions for everyone. This way, people felt like they had ownership over their own workspaces. We took votes several times along the way for important group decisions to create procedural fairness. It took some time and patience, but in the end the move went smoothly, and most people preferred the new office space.

There I was, sitting on the subway, drinking my rosé and thinking about that horrible meeting. I decided to stop feeling sorry for myself and start doing something about it. I found the only piece of paper I had in my purse and got to work. The first taxonomy of jerks was written while sitting next to a man in an Elvis suit listening to Queen and a woman with a chicken on her lap.

1

Kiss Up/Kick Downer

The first time I met Dave was during his informal lunch interview with my boss, Marie. I worked for a high-end department store, and Dave was transferring from another branch. He was tall and stylish, with a thick head of hair and a healthy five o'clock shadow. Legend had it that he had sold so many shoes at his previous location that he won a free car.

Marie was enthralled. Usually during job interviews, the interviewee tries to impress the boss. Not today. Marie didn't ask any questions. Instead, she layered on compliment after compliment.

"Everyone in Houston says wonderful things about you," she gushed.

"Well, I definitely didn't do it alone," Dave demurred. "A good team culture is critical for success."

Later, Marie asked me and two other salespeople to take Dave to dinner. We went to a delicious but tiny Italian restaurant that was famous for feeding only six people at a time. The table was probably meant for two but was set for four. Dave sat down first and immediately whisked one of the place settings to the other side. The three of us were left facing him like a squished panel of judges. "I want to see you when we talk," he said, smiling, elbows spread out wide, knees agape. Sandwiched between two men, I clenched my thighs together. I'm left-handed, so eating comfortably was out of the question.

Dinner was fine at first; everyone wanted to hear about how Dave won the car. But once we started talking to him as friends instead of as sycophants, he turned a bit sour. Having taken a three-week sommelier course in Napa, he insulted the real sommelier multiple times ("This is a cab *blend*, obviously"). He sent his dessert spoon back—not once but twice—because it was the wrong size.

The next day was Dave's first on the floor selling shoes. Whenever the regional manager was within earshot, Dave was lovely. He gently coached the newest salesperson on how to upsell a client, confident yet not overbearing. But as soon as the manager left, it was a different story.

I overheard him say to someone, "I'm worried about what Tessa is doing. Doesn't she know how to use a shoehorn?" I felt embarrassed.

It went from bad to worse thereafter. Left to his own devices, Dave would steal customers from other salespeople and rearrange shoes in the storage room so it was impossible to find anything (insisting, of course, that this was how shoes were arranged in the Houston store). We were all convinced that he hid the size tens from the rest of us. Ten is the most popular men's shoe size, and you can't make any money without size tens in stock.

When you're mean in retail, word gets around, so you can imagine my surprise when I walked into Marie's office for our monthly check-in and she hit me with an enthusiastic, "Hasn't Dave been so great! His sales are through the roof. He also raved about how wonderful it has been working with you and the other team members." Marie was socially adept and had a good radar for troublemakers and "shoe sharks" (people who steal customers from other salespeople). But clearly Dave had convinced her that he was the whole package: good with customers, good with the sales team.

Over time, Dave came to be known as the "kiss up/kick down" shoe guy. His charming personality and quick wit made him an easy sell to the store managers, and his numbers were so strong there was no denying his talent. But he was competitive and Machiavellian, willing to do anything to get ahead. Dave was causing me emotional strife and costing me sales, and no one with power seemed to know it.

I had to do something.

WINNER TAKE ALL

Kiss up/kick down coworkers have a singular goal in mind: to climb to the top by any means necessary. To get there, they treat everyone who is at the same level or below them as competition. They reserve their good manners for the people in charge.

There's a personality trait called *social comparison orientation*— it's the degree to which we naturally compare ourselves with other people. We all have the trait, but some of us more than others. When I worked in retail, I compared my sales numbers with Dave's. I've stalked the social media accounts of people from high school to see how much better off their lives are than mine. But I usually know when to quit; worrying about how much richer, hotter, and happier other people are is a dangerous game to play with oneself.

Kiss up/kick downers can't turn off the switch; they obsessively compare themselves with everyone, especially similar people. If you have the same job title, pedigree, or, hell, even the same size office as a kiss up/kick downer, beware; they're probably sizing you up regularly. Watch out for people who know just a little too much about you—down to the penny of your last raise, or how many more months (or days) they've been at the job than you. Social comparison sleuths like these use their knowledge to devise clever and devastating methods of competition. Some, like Dave, will question your expertise with your coworkers or raise small concerns with the boss.

This strategy, however, isn't without risk. Imagine if Dave had insulted someone like my coworker JW—shoe salesperson extraordinaire with zero tolerance for below-the-belt tactics and a bit of an anger issue. Dave would have wound up shining shoes during peak sales hours instead of working the floor, watching his back when he walked to his car at night.

But he didn't. And if your kiss up/kick downer knows what he's doing, neither will he.

Dave, like many of his kind, had another skill at his disposal: he knew how to read a room. He could walk into a sales meeting of top executives and make a ton of observations—where people sat, who talked without being interrupted, who smiled at whom, and who shaped the direction of the conversation. This skill—which my colleagues Siyu Yu and Gavin Kilduff and I call *status acuity*—helps kiss up/kick downers figure out not only whom they should compare themselves with but whom they can safely criticize to those in power.

It turns out this skill is quantifiable. In a study, Siyu, Gavin, and I had people watch groups of strangers work together for about ninety seconds and then rank who they thought was the most respected by their group members and who was the least. When we compared these ratings with the actual group members' ratings, we found something surprising. Not only were some people quite good at the task, but when we retested them a year or so later, their scores were virtually unchanged. In other words, status acuity is a skill that stays with us.

It didn't take Dave long to rank order people at work, and it didn't take long for him to figure out who the safe targets were. He knew immediately that JW was a threat, but he was smart enough not to sabotage him.

Sneaky behaviors to watch out for

They belittle you in front of the people you're trying to impress. Kiss up/kick downers start out small, often with little comments meant to question your expertise. ("Do you *really* know how to impress that client? I thought you only had two months' experience.")

They reserve the nastiest behavior for one-on-one time. Expect small acts of sabotage, such as hidden shoes, that a kiss up/kick downer can plausibly deny. Condescending comments, inappropriate favor asking, and misdirection are also on the menu, anything to make you feel less at home at work.

They offer favors to overworked and overwhelmed bosses.
If your boss needs a job done off-hours, someone to interview
the new interns in their spare time, or someone to serve on
that dreaded committee, expect your kiss up/kick downer to
step up.

They approach high-power people outside of work.
Exclusive company parties, workout classes, soccer games,
and the grocery store are all fair game! Kiss up/kick downers
are opportunists who think outside of the box. If there's a
chance to press the flesh outside the workplace, they'll find it.

WHY DO THEY NEED TO KICK DOWN?

Kissing up and kicking down is a time-consuming and risky strategy, which begs the question, why do it in the first place?

For starters, competition at the top is stiff, and it's going to only
get worse over time. In a recent Mercer survey, 90 percent of C-suite
execs said they expect talent competition to increase in the coming few years. For those who make it, the perks might be well worth
the effort. According to economist Robert Frank, rewards for top
jobs at companies such as Netflix and Goldman Sachs aren't just
massive, they are substantially greater than those at companies
just one tier down. And in companies that thrive on a scarcity
mind-set—only a handful of people will ever make it to the top—
employees are often encouraged to fight among themselves to get

ahead by any means necessary. The "do it whatever it takes" mantra is directly communicated to people, often by their bosses, who brag about those who got to where they are by exploiting naïve or "weak" people. But beyond being a means to an end, kissing up and kicking down serve a surprising purpose—it helps people like Dave reduce their stress at work.

Why?

People like Dave are attracted to competitive jungles—they like working in places where the CEO makes five hundred times as much as entry-level employees. They are high on what scientists call *social dominance orientation*. Believe it or not, some people, such as kiss up/kick downers, love hierarchies, even if they're at the bottom. You would be hard-pressed to find a kiss up/kick downer who chose to work in a place that had a flat structure, where everyone makes about the same amount of money and has about the same amount of power. And in their competitive jungles, kiss up/kick downers like a challenge: they want to be the CEO who makes five hundred times as much as the new guy.

Unfortunately for a lot of us—including the Daves of the world—power is a precarious thing. In a lot of jobs (such as retail), transfers are common and often beyond our control. After the pandemic, offices closed left and right. Even if you're able to work for the same company, there's a good chance you will be transferred to another location. Dave was happy to transfer from the Houston store, where his bad reputation had caught up with him, but he still had to start all over, reasserting his power and relearning the status hierarchy.

Kiss up/kick downers quickly figure out that the best way to reduce their stress is to solidify their position of power early and hold on to it by any means necessary, even if that means destroying the people around them. For them, kissing up is a strategy that secures their power in an uncertain world and reduces the stress they feel about losing that power.

This is one case where the tactics people use to reduce stress at work cause collateral damage.

STRENGTHS AND WEAKNESSES

Competitive work environments are like sub-Saharan Africa. There are a lot of animals fighting for apex status, all of whom use different tactics to hunt their prey. Some hunt quietly, sneaking up on their victim when they least expect it. Others are powerful runners. Kiss up/kick downers are no different.

You need to learn their strengths and weaknesses.

THEY GRAB POWER EARLY

I remember the first time I witnessed someone quietly and effectively become the most powerful person in the room. It was during a job search, and the committee was sluggishly moving through the process. The first day of our meeting I walked into the room and saw a big stack of job candidate packets on a table, next to a half-eaten tray of cookies.

Only the cookies were getting attention.

After about five minutes of mindless chatter, my coworker Mark got antsy. "How about we start by ordering the candidate packets alphabetically. I will review A through D. Tessa, you can review E through I, and so on. Sound good?" In that moment,

Mark became the leader. It was a seamless and uncontested assertion of power.

Years later, my colleagues Katherine Thorson, Oana Dumitru, and I designed a series of studies to formally test what I observed that day. We had groups of five strangers work together to choose a job candidate. Unbeknownst to the rest of the group, we approached one group member before the session started and told her that if she could successfully persuade the group to pick a particular candidate (whom we chose at random), we would give her extra money. The catch was, she couldn't tell anyone.

We know from the science of persuasion that argument quality matters. Kate, Oana, and I assumed this finding would bear out in our study too, but we were wrong. Instead, our results mirrored what I had observed in Mark a few years back. Successful persuaders were those who asserted themselves at the beginning of the interaction. The simple act of saying to the group, "Let's start by going around and saying our names" was enough to get the job done. From then on, the group turned to this person for guidance.

There's a phenomenon in education called the *Matthew effect*: if you learn something early in life like reading, it's much easier to build on your skills and become good at that thing than if you try to learn it later in life. Power at work operates the same way. Gaining a little bit of power early is a much better strategy than gaining a lot of it late.

Kiss up/kick downers don't want to fit themselves into the existing power structure; they want to help build it. Beware of coworkers who sneak their way into roles that on the surface don't seem to come with much power. Even jobs such as group organizer can give a kiss up/kick downer that foothold they need to become power players down the road.

THEY FIND COMMONALITIES WITH
PEOPLE IN POWER

When you work in sales, meetings often resemble cheerleading pep rallies ("We are in it to win it!" is thrown around without the least bit of irony). It's just the nature of the business. Some people get really into it; I never did. At my shoe job we had a big pep rally once a year when everyone got together to hear about the latest products. Buyers, product reps, managers, and salespeople all attended.

For Dave, these meetings provided a critical opportunity to kiss up to powerful people he wouldn't see again until the next pep rally.

One year I was late, so I hid behind a big holiday display so my boss wouldn't see me. From my hiding spot I caught Dave chatting up a store manager, the two of them laughing their asses off like high schoolers planning a prank on the substitute. What could be so funny? To find out, I snuck over and eavesdropped. To my surprise, Dave and the manager were talking about how hilarious it was that they were wearing the same pair of designer jeans. What a coincidence!

Dave probably planned it.

We know that similarity breeds liking, but just how incidental can these similarities be to work? Dave managed to build rapport with someone over jeans. My collaborator Joe Magee and I found that people can also build rapport over similar answers to "Would You Rather" dilemmas. In a series of studies, we had people answer seven questions such as "Would you rather fly or be invisible?" and "Would you rather walk ten miles or run two?" Half of the people were told they had five out of seven answers in common with a future interaction partner, and half were told they had only two in common. (We lied about this part. Actual similarity doesn't matter; people just need to believe they are similar.) Once they met, those in the five group had better rapport and worked better together as a team than those in the two group.

Gaining power isn't always about kissing ass, it's also about finding the one thing that will get people in power to warm up to you. Being too sycophantic can be irritating, but commonalities work on everyone.

BUT THEY CAN ALSO BE SHORTSIGHTED

Kiss up/kick down coworkers have a skill set that should not be underestimated. But sorting people into loser and winner groups ultimately amounts to thinking about people instrumentally— what can they do for you *right now*? This strategy might work in the short term, but status is not a stable thing. It can flux and flow as people move around and take on different roles at work.

Think about the modern workplace environment. Many companies now offer office rotation options where you work between offices. The National Football League's Junior Rotational Program allows you to work in four different locations over a four-year period (New York, California, DC, and New Jersey). Programs such as these create contact between employees who traditionally would never interact. Gossip spreads quickly, and people who kick down risk serious damage to their reputation. Kiss up/kick down coworkers run a real risk by abusing people who they might one day need to rely on, or who could even become their boss.

WHERE DO THEY DO IT?

To be successful, kiss up/kick down coworkers need to divide and conquer. It's bit like pulling off two relationships at the same time, where neither lover knows the other one exists. Preferably, your two lovers don't have overlapping social circles. And if they do have a chance encounter, you'd better damn well have a plan.

Therefore, kiss up/kick downers spend a lot of time orchestrating that plan. To prepare for the possibility that someone will eventually complain about them, they work hard to forge connections with powerful people who can protect them.

ALONE WITH THE BOSS

Often when we think about jerks at work, we blame our bosses. Why haven't they fired these people? Don't they care about workplace morale? We assume a direction of causality from boss to employee. But it can certainly be the other way around. Bosses can be the victims of toxic protégés—employees who engage in exploitative, deceptive behavior. Protégés such as kiss up/kick downers use the help, knowledge, and social connections of their mentors to get ahead. They also seek out bosses whom they can easily exploit.

And what types of bosses are these?

Bosses who are disconnected from their team members (such as the neglectful boss in chapter 6) and those who are eager to hand off responsibilities to conscientious go-getters make great targets. Kiss up/kick downers can control the narrative of how they behave at work; absentee bosses rarely fact-check. They also create dependency by doing the one thing most of us avoid: more work.

I once met a kiss up/kick downer, Sarah, who was the master of free labor. Anytime a new project cropped up, she would track down her neglectful boss and volunteer for it. Sarah never actually had the time to do the work, so she strong-armed her subordinates into doing it for her on the weekends. When the inevitable happened and the subordinates complained, Sarah's boss shrugged off the grumbling. Why should he care? Sarah made his life easier. With her boss on her side, Sarah slowly became a toxic protégé.

Don't get me wrong. Knowing how to delegate work properly is the marker of a good boss. The danger occurs when bosses delegate *everything* to kiss up/kick downers, including communication with their team. Once Sarah took on the role of press secretary, all bets were off; her boss no longer had a handle on how her behavior was affecting other people. Bosses should check in with all members of their teams—no matter how busy they are—to make sure conniving climbers don't go undetected.

AT SOCCER MATCHES AND SPIN CLASSES— ANYWHERE THEY CAN CATCH YOU UNAWARES

I once knew a clever kiss up/kick downer, Stella, who joined a "Saturday Surf Time" interest group because it was organized by a leader she couldn't get close to at work. Stella hated sand and slimy seaweed—she was a pool person, not a beach person. She also had very sensitive skin, and it wasn't long before she developed surfer's rash—gross red bumps you get from wearing a wet suit for too long. But Stella sucked it up, layered on the Vaseline, and went all-in on the surf club. Burning, itching skin was a small price to pay for a new connection.

Powerful people are busy and often difficult to reach. You could go your whole life working for a company and never meet the people at the top. Kiss up/kick downers find a workaround; they go outside the workplace to press the flesh.

Some connect with the powerful to make themselves known, others to control your reputation. And the smart ones know not to stalk their boss but someone at arm's length, such as their boss's boss or her best buddy from college, to damage you with higher-ups.

Why?

Basically, it's easier to control someone else's reputation at a distance. People two steps removed from you don't know you very well and probably don't have a strong opinion about you—good or bad— that your kiss up/kick downer would have to contend with. Two, if they screw up and gossip to someone who likes you, the damage can be controlled. The farther away people are from us at work, the less likely they are to care about our inappropriate workplace behavior. I get more upset when my direct reports do something unprofessional than my colleague's direct reports; only mine can make me look bad. And if the juicy tidbits planted by the kiss up/ kick downer are worth spreading, your boss will eventually get the message.

Indirect strategies are often the most effective ones in getting ahead at work.

Kiss up/kick downers are skilled jerks at work; they can read a room and they know how to get powerful people to like them. But by far their best skill is their ability to poison the well against you. Should you march into your boss's office to complain, chances are you will be met with eye rolls and accusations of jealousy (I was, but more on that below). You need to think strategically to beat them at their own game.

Start with paying careful attention to the warning signs, such as chronic and inappropriate social comparisons. Next, you will need to enlist the help of your social network to collect evidence of mistreatment. Lastly, you will need to approach your boss carefully, keeping in mind that by this point, they probably have fondness for your enemy. As you move through the process, do not underestimate the amount of time and effort your kiss up/kick downer is putting into their strategy. The most talented among them have built a strong reputation with the powerful people you need to persuade. They will also come prepared with an enviable skill set.

GOAL 1: FIND A WELL-CONNECTED ALLY TO GIVE YOU PERSPECTIVE

The first time I was kicked down at work, I questioned my experience. "Am I being too sensitive? Is this just the way people compete here?" I didn't know what stepping over the line looked like. Kiss up/kick downers take advantage of naïve people like me.

Allies give you a reality check. The best ones aren't the people you go to for emotional support; they are the people who work at arm's length from you. Your goal is to find someone who is connected broadly and widely within your social network; someone who knows a lot of people, even if just superficially, at many levels of the organization. Your ally can give you an accurate picture of how widespread your jerk-at-work problem is.

Now you might be thinking, "Only powerful people are well-connected at work." Not so. In fact, the people who have the most network ties—connections to lots of people across the organization—often don't hold positions of power at all. In terrorist organizations, these are the taxi drivers and the people who transport goods from one location to another.

In my retail job, my ally was Jamal. He worked in the department store coffee shop. Jamal knew everyone, from the top executives who stopped by once a year to the plainclothes police officers who monitored for shoplifters. And because people gossip over coffee, his mental map of people's reputations rivaled that of the most talented kiss up/kick downers. I asked Jamal if he had heard anything about Dave, good or bad (don't just seek out self-confirming evidence). It turns out that Dave was terrorizing a lot of people, not just me. My first goal was accomplished; I learned that the Dave problem was widespread.

GOAL 2: FIND OTHER TARGETS

The next step is to find other people who've also been targeted by your kiss up/kick downer. If you're feeling a bit sheepish about this stage of the process, you're not alone. People hate awkward social interactions; the potential to hear "no" might be enough to scare you away.

Keep a few things in mind when you approach people. One, your goal is not to convince them your kiss up/kick downer is a bad person; you aren't here to smear Dave's reputation. I like to open these conversations with something neutral: "Have you interacted much with Dave? How's that been?" Once someone admits to also being targeted, feel free to share your experiences. Stick with the facts and avoid personal attacks; the key is that you don't sacrifice professionalism during this conversation. If the person is comfortable opening up to you, ask if they are willing to speak to the boss with you or, if not, if they give you permission to mention their experience to the boss. Write down what they say and have them go over it with you.

Two, keep in mind that not everyone will be willing to step forward, even if they've had bad experiences. Some might be inadvertent enablers—they would rather turn a blind eye because they are overwhelmed, they worry about retaliation, or they aren't motivated enough to care. Some might be allies with your kiss up/kick downer, willing to go along for the ride if it means they can gain some power too one day.

Three, there's a chance your kiss up/kick downer will get wind of what you're trying to do, so expect some counterattacks. Ask your ally for guidance on whom it would be best to approach. If you get enough hard data—actual evidence of mistreatment— then you should be in a strong position moving forward. The data you collect should be detailed and focused on the facts. Concentrate on what the kiss up/kick downer did, not on how you feel about what they did. The more detailed the better.

GOAL 3: BUFFER

You'll need to create physical and psychological buffers between you and your kiss up/kick downer to help reduce stress throughout this process. Start by writing down how often and when you have face-to-face contact with this person. This might feel silly, but there's a surprising number of daily interactions we have with people that we forget about (such as in the elevator, for instance). Are these interactions things you can plan for, such as a weekly meeting, or ones you can't plan for, such as run-ins by the coffee machine? If you can plan for the interaction, ask allies to help you create physical distance. My research has found that simply sitting a few feet away from someone can reduce anxiety. If you must sit at a table with this person, sit on the same side, at least two people away. Reducing the likelihood of eye contact will make you feel more in control.

GOAL 4: APPROACH YOUR SUPERVISOR

The first time I got up the gumption to talk to Marie about Dave, it didn't go over as planned. "Dave is disrespectful to others, he lies, and he blocks my sales," I blurted out. The moment the words came out of my mouth I saw the warmth drain from Marie's face.

"I was afraid this was happening," she told me. "Dave said that you've been acting really competitive with him. He thinks you might feel threatened by his success. Look, Tessa, Dave really wants to get along with you. I know he brings talents to this team that quite frankly the rest of you don't have, but I don't have tolerance for petty jealousy right now. This isn't high school."

I walked away, my tail between my legs.

What I failed to appreciate is that by the time I felt justified in complaining, Marie and Dave had formed a bond. Dave made Marie's life easier, her sales numbers stronger. The next time I talked to Marie, I took a different approach. As much as it pained me, I opened by acknowledging Dave's strengths. Denying his talent only made me look resentful.

"I know things are going really great with Dave in the sales department," I said. "No one can upsell a client quite like Dave. And the customers love him."

She waited for the "but."

"But I'm a little worried about our work environment," I said, emphasizing the "our." "And I don't think it's just me. A handful of people are having some issues with him. I'm a little worried that if things don't improve, some of our top talent might leave."

This was Marie's biggest fear.

From there, I laid out a few examples of Dave's behavior, emphasizing that she should talk to others to hear their perspectives. At this point she was relying on Dave for information about her team, and I didn't want her to do the same with me.

I focused less on how people felt about Dave and more on his specific actions. Marie wasn't thrilled to hear me criticize Dave, but she wasn't totally resistant to it either, which was good enough for me.

When it comes to talking to your boss, reducing the perception that you're vindictive or jealous will go a long way toward establishing your credibility. Bosses are more receptive if there's a pattern of bad behavior than if there's a conflict between two people.

GOAL 5: WAIT

Once I was done talking with Marie, I had to sit back and wait.

In my experience, waiting is the hardest part of the process.

Recently, a dean at New York University (NYU) told me, "Just because you don't see action happening doesn't mean the wheels aren't turning behind the scenes. Be patient. Power players often can't disclose details. It violates privacy laws." To this day I need to remind myself of this advice. Be patient and give your boss time before you prod them again.

A BOSS'S GUIDE TO PREVENTING KISS UP/KICK DOWN BEHAVIOR

As I gained power and status, I learned that competition is sometimes unavoidable, especially in jobs in which a very small minority will make it to the top. These environments are highly susceptible to kiss up/kick downers. As a boss, you should follow a few steps to make the ground less fertile for them to grow.

One, avoid giving leadership roles to people who haven't earned the respect of their coworkers, particularly those who work at the same level or below them. Don't trust your own instincts regarding who would be good for these jobs; ask around.

Two, put small safeguards in place that prevent kiss up/kick downers from taking advantage of new employees who don't yet know the ropes. Dave routinely stole customers from new salespeople, so Marie started a rule that we would rotate customers. (I got one, then Dave, then the new guy, etc.) Fairness norms are a good way to block kick-down behavior.

Three, stay connected to all your team members; don't rely on one or two people who work under you to communicate with everyone else on your behalf. Treating a kiss up/kick downer as your personal assistant is the biggest gift you can give them. Remember, kiss up/kick downers thrive when the people they kiss up to are cut off from those they kick down.

Before you go

Kiss up/kick down coworkers have a singular goal in mind: to climb to the top by any means necessary.

▶ They come to the workplace with a set of skills, including the ability to read a room. Kiss up/kick downers can tell—simply by observing how people behave toward one another—who has status and who does not.

▶ To form connections with powerful people, kiss up/kick downers will engage in all sorts of tactics, including finding small commonalities with them, to break the ice.

▶ When it comes to gaining power at work, the early bird gets the worm. Kiss up/kick downers assert themselves before status hierarchies are established.

▶ It's not hard to find a kiss up/kick downer in action, if you know where to look. They will have more meetings with the boss and show up to more opportunistic events (such as interest groups) than everyone else.

▶ To beat a kiss up/kick downer, follow a few steps. First, find allies who aren't friends or confidants. Allies are well-connected people who will help give you a reality check.

▶ Second, find others who've been targeted by your kiss up/kick downer. Be careful when you approach people; don't assume they are on your side.

▶ Third, create psychological and physical distance from your kiss up/kick downer. Even moving a few chairs over in a meeting can help reduce your stress.

▶ Fourth, before you meet with your boss, collect detailed data on your experiences. Make your report about your kiss up/kick downer's behaviors, not about your feelings.

▶ Fifth, after you meet with your boss, be patient and wait. Real change takes time.

▶ If you are the boss, create rules that give everyone an equal shot. These rules will reduce the likelihood that people will kiss up and kick down to get ahead.

2

The Credit Stealer

Sandra knew that working in real estate wasn't for the faint of heart. The last person she knew who tried it and failed was Kara, her college roommate. Charismatic and polished, Kara had the trappings of a successful broker. But she was sensitive—quick to cry if someone was rude to her or gossiped about her behind her back. Real estate ate her alive. Now she was fostering rescue puppies for a living.

Sandra, on the other hand, was as gritty as they come. She had an MBA from an Ivy League school and survived ten years working in finance. "If I can handle finance bros, I can handle anything," she reasoned to herself. She breezed through the real estate license exam and got a job working under the tutelage of Jose, the best broker in Southern California.

Jose was slick.

He dressed like a Bel Air plastic surgeon—bespoke three-piece suits, Italian loafers, expensive smile. At six foot three with caramel skin and a muscular build, everyone thought he was a model. And he was, six years ago.

When the two first met, Jose was giddy with excitement. "An Ivy Leaguer has come to real estate? We are going to kill it together!"

And they did. Within the first six months, Jose helped Sandra sell five homes over the $5 million mark—unheard-of for a first-time broker. He also got her on the radar of the top foreign investors. Sandra was catching up to Jose quickly. It made him nervous.

The theft started out slowly—an idea here, a listing there. First, Jose stole Sandra's idea to stage a beach house in all-white furniture. "I know it sounds tacky, but everyone else is using the same nouveau riche look," Sandra mentioned over brunch. Jose waved away the idea, but a few days later, he rented all the high-end white furniture within a thirty-mile radius for his own showing. She was left with nothing but plastic lawn chairs.

Next, he "borrowed" Sandra's negotiation tactics—which she honestly was okay with—until he used them on her clients. "I figured you wouldn't mind if I handled the Thomases this time around, you seemed swamped," he told her. Sandra stiffened. The Thomases were notoriously finicky buyers, and it had taken her a year to get them to trust her.

From Sandra's perspective, the worst part about the theft was that there was always enough ambiguity for Jose to deny it. "You didn't invent the concept of all white," Jose barked. "And the Thomases were my clients long before you came along. You don't own people in real estate."

Sandra felt bested and humiliated: she couldn't leave the brokerage and step out on her own; she certainly wasn't ready to move to a new city and build her client base up from scratch; and if she worked for a competitor, Jose would surely retaliate.

Her only choice, it seemed, was to continue to let Jose suck the blood out of her, like a vampire bat snacking on livestock; not enough blood was drawn to kill her, but it was certainly enough to weaken her. Those rescue puppies were sounding better and better.

WOLVES IN SHEEP'S CLOTHING

Credit stealing is one of the most common causes of conflict at work. Yet, despite our wealth of experience being theft victims, we are surprisingly inept at recognizing the warning signs.

Why? Because we're looking for them in all the wrong places. Most of us worry about theft coming from the outside. About 50 percent of companies have employees sign noncompete contracts to prevent them from sharing company secrets when they quit. But the reality is, employees are more likely to steal from companies they still work for. A surprising 25 percent of people have committed expense fraud at work, like claiming that a travel dinner cost a hundred bucks when it cost only fifty. About half of people have had an idea stolen at work by someone trying to look good.

Credit stealing is an intimate form of workplace theft—it is not done by strangers but by our teammates, mentees, and ostensible friends. Credit stealers are the people who encourage you come to them when you have a half-baked idea that needs working through, the kiss up/kick downer who feigns interest in helping you thrive, or the mentor who becomes jealous of your success. Because we know and trust them, credit stealers are able to exploit our vulnerability and use it to their advantage.

The theft usually starts out small, like an idea to use all-white furniture. Smart credit stealers test the waters first to see how much theft they can get away with. Vulnerable victims, such as Sandra, have little choice but to continue working with credit stealers. And the more respect they've earned among their senior coworkers, the more likely they are to get away with it. Well-connected ones such as Jose work their way up to stealing big ideas and breakthroughs with almost no concerns about being called out. They masterfully cover their tracks, leaving enough wiggle room to deny it later. And in the end, accusations of credit stealing are often met with eye rolls and refusals to take sides.

Sneaky behaviors to watch out for

Credit stealers are opportunists. If you're working on a team, they wait for moments of ambiguity to take credit for your ideas or work. Think group meetings, company lunches, and informal feedback sessions—all places where no one is keeping track of who did what.

You will know your credit stealer, and well. Credit stealers are mentees, allies, and so-called friends. New bosses who feel threatened by your success and competitive team members are likely candidates. Credit stealing is also a favored strategy of the kiss up/kick downer.

Credit stealers take advantage of vulnerable bosses. Bosses who make more money, land more clients, or gain power when their team members successfully steal credit make great targets.

Not all credit stealing is intentional. Credit stealers can be regular folks—such as you and me—who have biases that make them overestimate their role in decision-making. What feels toxic to us feels justified to them.

Knowing what to do about credit stealing depends on where it's happening—is it during a group meeting where ideas are "in the air," or one-on-one, as with Sandra and Jose? The first half of this chapter is dedicated to showing you how to combat intentional credit stealing in intimate workplace settings, such as between mentors and mentees or between two peers. Looking out for red flags is important, but so too is making sure that the right people support you when you make contributions, so that when you speak up other people listen.

The second half of this chapter will show you how to navigate credit stealing in teams, where the solutions involve changing the process by which teams operate *before* the work starts. By the end of this chapter, you'll be able to confront a credit stealer and learn how to prevent credit stealing from happening again.

WHEN CREDIT STEALING IS UP CLOSE AND PERSONAL

Often at work, there is no ambiguity around who did the work or who came up with the idea. You did, and you should get credit for it. Worried about intentional credit stealing? Here are the most common culprits.

FOES DISGUISED AS FRIENDS

In the natural world, lots of animals have figured out that would-be friends make the best theft targets. There are probably millions of years of evolution behind this strategy.

Take, for example, the male scorpionfly. To get a female to mate with him, he needs to bring her a dead bug as a postcoital snack. But juicy bugs are hard to find, and the smart flies steal theirs from un-suspecting males by pretending to be females. The strategy works. Male flies that pirate their prey have a lot more sex partners, and make a lot more babies, than those that don't.

Smart credit stealers aren't that far removed from male scorpion-flies: they steal from unsuspecting coworkers who are close to them. And the smart ones never get caught.

Sandra, the ill-fated real estate broker, serves as a cautionary example.

After a few years working with Jose, Sandra finally had enough. Jose had reclaimed the Thomas family and closed on the biggest sale of the year: a cliffside mansion overlooking the bluffs of Mal-ibu. To celebrate, he rented a yacht and invited all the top brokers for an upscale booze cruise.

Champagne in hand, Jose launched into a self-congratulatory speech. But just when Sandra was ready to chuck his well-defined body into the Pacific, he thew her a curveball: he *gave* her credit for something she didn't really do.

"If it wasn't for Sandra, I never would have closed this deal," he told the crowd. "She's the glue that held it all together." Sandra had nothing to do with the sale—she had been off feeling sorry for herself in Barbados when the whole thing went down. Why would Jose do this?

Lest you think your credit stealer is a one-trick pony, think again. Clever credit stealers don't always overclaim credit—sometimes they underclaim it. Why?

According to UC Berkeley's Daniel Stein, people adjust their credit claims to meet different impression-management goals. They overclaim contributions to appear competent and to attract others to work with them, and they underclaim them to appear humble. For people like Jose, who play dirty in their own backyard, this strategy can prevent them from getting caught. Just when Sandra was ready to call him out, Jose did something that would have made her look unhinged and ungrateful—gave her very public credit for something she didn't do.

Most credit stealers who underclaim credit do so in group settings: during thank-you speeches, feedback sessions with leaders, and onboarding sessions. They like to create the impression that they are team players. Like the kiss up/kick downer, the stealing goes on behind closed doors, when no one else is watching.

THE BOSS WHO GETS A KICKBACK

Part of the responsibility of a boss is to stop credit stealing from happening, right? I like to think so. Before I started writing this book, I struggled to understand why any boss would enable it. Sure, some bosses are intimidated by credit stealers, so they don't intervene, but eventually the chickens will come home to roost. You can't let that shit go on forever.

Then I learned of a special category of bosses—those who don't just allow credit stealing to go unchecked, they help make it happen.

Consider the case of Kiddy, an interior designer with weak talent but strong connections to the art world.

Kiddy's boss, Tal, ran a boutique firm that catered to the ultra-wealthy. He was eager to use Kiddy's connections, so he hired her, then showered her with praise for things she didn't do to keep her happy.

Tal was working hard to impress a client at an art exhibit. "It was Kiddy's idea to use gold filigree wallpaper in the master bath. A genius move, if you ask me," he told them. Kiddy blushed. "I really felt myself growing in that moment, using color and texture in new and unexpected ways," she said.

Kiddy didn't come up with the wallpaper idea—a newcomer named June did—but why correct Tal? The accolades felt good. Over time, Kiddy and Tal got into a nice little routine. Her team would come up ideas, she would get credit for them, and in return, Tal used Kiddy's connections to secure art for his clients. They were the shark and remora of the design world.

Then one day, a very fussy client arrived.

Marc learned of Kiddy's reputation through some art friends, and he was eager to see what she could do to spice up his country property. Marc was a private man, and he hated the thought of the design team crawling about his space like busy little ants. So only Kiddy was given the keys. He also hated the sound of multiple voices on a call, so only Kiddy was allowed to phone him. At the one-month mark, Kiddy had purchased two sculptures by an up-and-coming artist for the loft space, and that was it.

She hadn't so much as picked a paint color for the garage.

Realizing that rumors of Kiddy's talent had been greatly exaggerated, Marc was furious. Kiddy got fired, and Tal's reputation was in tatters.

Sometimes, the person who suffers the most from credit stealing isn't the victim—it's the kickback boss who has something to gain from it. If you work for a boss like Tal and there's a Kiddy on your team, get off the team as quickly as you can. Unless you have very strong connections with people who can overrule your boss, you probably will never get credit for your ideas. Yes, your boss knows what you contributed, but that's irrelevant; they have their own selfish reasons for enabling credit stealing. And when credit stealing is endorsed by the boss, it spreads like wildfire. Bad behavior at work is contagious.

CULTIVATE YOUR VOICE

At some point, you will likely be targeted by a credit stealer. This is especially true if you work in a competitive organization where your worth is judged by what you produce. Like other jerks at work, intentional credit stealers build up to the egregious stuff. Some slowly eat away at zero-sum resources, such as client lists. Others "borrow" ideas they initially feigned interest in. And when they interact with powerful people, they pretend to be generous credit sharers.

It's important to look out for red flags and early warning signs, but if you want to get credit for your contributions at work, the single most important thing you can do is have more "voice" than your credit stealer. I mean this literally and figuratively. Your credit stealer probably talks louder than you, but they might also have status and power, which means that when they speak, people listen.

Voice is a combination of a few things. It means that when you speak up, other people stop speaking and turn their attention to you. It also means that after you say something important, people attribute your idea to you, and no one else, long after you've said it.

The trick to creating a voice for yourself is to become respected by your coworkers and your boss *before* you walk into the room; it is tough to gain voice in a meeting without doing some behind-the-scenes work first. People whose bosses and coworkers grant them voice rise up the ladder quickly. They don't waste time battling credit stealers because they don't have to.

I knew a boss, Blaine, who was going through a bad divorce. Every Monday for about three months Blaine met with his lawyers for two hours in the morning. He was always in a bad mood afterward.

Blaine was notoriously tough to pin down, so new employees were pleasantly surprised when they learned of two magically free hours in his schedule every Monday from eleven a.m. to one p.m. Those who were lucky enough to know his favorite team member, Kai, knew not to snag the Monday window. "Never meet with Blaine after those lawyer meetings. Hold off for another day of the week—even if that means having to wait an extra ten days," Kai told them.

Kai was well-connected at work and full of little nuggets of advice. She could tell you which senior leaders Blaine respected the most (and which he respected the least), who in the office could charm the most difficult clients, and which holiday parties were best to avoid.

Blaine was a busy man—he didn't have time to go door-to-door asking different people for advice about different things. Instead, he relied on a handful of people to keep him in the loop, and he granted them voice. Kai was one of them.

And once she was granted voice, she was recognized for her

ideas and hard work. Credit stealers didn't dare try stealing from Kai; they knew Blaine would immediately shoot them down.

How did Kai get there?

In the largest study of voice recognition to date, Taeya Howell and her colleagues studied more than one thousand employees to ask the question, What does it take to have voice at work? The best predictor of having voice was being known as an *advice tie*—someone others go to for advice on how to get ahead.

The best way to become an advice tie is to learn from other advice ties. From the moment she was hired, Kai went out of her way to find out who the people were in the organization who knew how to get things done. The first week on the job, she had coffee with several people ranging from office staff to long-standing employees, all of whom could tell her different things about her work environment. One person knew when the president of the company came to the office ("Don't ask for anything that week"), another knew whom Blaine turned to for advice and whom he had an ongoing conflict with. By connecting with different types of employees, Kai was able to develop a broad social network.

Next, Kai observed how Blaine and other senior leaders behaved in meetings when other people shared their ideas. Who was listened to and who was ignored? Was Blaine receptive to people who cut others off, or annoyed by them? Learning what works and what doesn't—which varies a bit from person to person—is an important skill to acquire.

Once Kai started to develop a wealth of knowledge of how to successfully navigate the workplace, she was generous with offering advice to others. To become an advice tie yourself, it's important not only to have useful information, but also to be willing to share with it others. Hoarding it all to yourself won't do you much good.

As Kai learned, advice ties at work aren't necessarily the most accomplished or powerful people. They may already be in our social groups—we recognize them from a party, or we were on a team with them before. I recommend building a network of advice ties who have different types of insider knowledge (you don't want a group of ten people who all know your boss's dirty little secrets but not much else). Good advice ties can tell you when to ask for a meeting with the boss ("He's most responsive to requests that are two weeks out" or "It's either going to happen in forty-eight hours or never, so clear your schedule"), when to approach people and when to avoid them, and who has conflict with whom. I also love an advice tie who has a good sense of my boss's calendar—when are they too overwhelmed to help (such as the end of the fiscal year), when do they go on vacation, and what days of the week are they most able to squeeze me in.

In chapter 1, I talk about how to find well-connected allies—people who have a lot of relationships with other people in your social network and many weak ties (people they don't know well but who might be able to help you). These same people can also help you find advice ties. Many of them make great advice ties themselves.

DON'T CONFUSE ADVICE TIES WITH FRIENDSHIP TIES

One strategy you might be tempted to use to gain more advice ties is to ramp up your prosocial behavior. Perhaps you offer to go on coffee runs for busy people or throw your coworker Talia her baby shower. A little prosociality is a good thing, but too much of it can take away from your productivity at work. You won't be known as the person who knows how to get things done, you will be known as the person who is willing to take on jobs no one else is volunteering for.

Having a lot of friendship ties will not grant you voice at work. In fact, friendship ties can backfire. Taeya Howell found that the more friendship ties people had, the less voice recognition they got at work—especially if they were chatterboxes. Bosses don't love it when people spend time at work gossiping or making weekend plans—it distracts from getting real work done.

The solution, I should hope, isn't to stop socializing at work. Instead, try to keep the non-work-related chatter outside the office. You can have lots of advice ties and friendship ties, but the key is knowing when it's appropriate to use them.

CONTRIBUTE SOLUTIONS, NOT PROBLEMS

When people speak up in a meeting with the boss or during a group discussion, they usually make one of two types of contributions: they bring up problems or they bring up solutions.

Both seem relevant to gaining power and status with your peers, but it turns out that being focused on solutions works better. People prefer to listen to ideas of how the group can get ahead, not to what is holding them back. Once your peers give you status, then they start going to you for advice. Eventually your boss will get wind of your reputation and grant you voice.

RECOGNIZE THE UNSUNG HEROES, AND ECHO OTHERS WHO CONTRIBUTE

At work, you might witness others on your team get shortchanged in the credit-receiving department. Be an ally and give credit to people who aren't getting the recognition they deserve. Also, think creatively about what it takes to see a project to fruition and make sure all members of the team, not just the ones who take center stage, get credit. Making sure the right people are heard is just as important in combating credit stealing at work as weeding out individual credit stealers.

CONFRONTING THE CREDIT STEALER

I once gave a talk on a panel with two other people on how to make people feel comfortable speaking up at work. Every time I made a comment, one of the other panelists would basically say what I said, about thirty seconds later, acting as if my thoughts were his.

It became comical.

Luckily for me, I didn't have to confront him myself; someone in the audience did.

"Can you please stop repeated everything Tessa says, a few seconds after she says it? We don't need to hear her perspective twice."

Everyone sat in silence, unsure of what to do.

I broke the silence with a loud, awkward laugh that I put so much of my body into, my mic disconnected from its battery pack. In attempting to reconnect the two, I nearly fell out of my chair. My shoe fell off.

Confronting credit stealers is awkward business.

There is so much that could go wrong. But the key is to avoid being overly inflammatory—at least at first—so that you can move past this moment instead of letting it define your relationship with your jerk at work.

I like to plan my confrontations carefully and give myself control over the timing of their delivery (it was not fun for me, or my credit stealer, to have him called out in public). And like a lot of advice I give in this book, my plan starts by taking the perspective of my credit stealer when sharing mine.

STEP 1: SHARE YOUR PERSPECTIVE

Not all credit stealers are intentionally trying to sabotage you. Most probably think they deserve at least some ownership over the idea or the work. Instead of accusing your credit stealer of stealing—which will immediately make them defensive—share your perspective on what happened (and yes, use that word). You might say something like, "I noticed that in that meeting, the two of us were sharing pretty similar ideas. What's your perspective? Did you feel that way too? I felt like I usually contributed thoughts first, but what was your take on what happened?" This conversation might feel like that argument you had with your spouse or roommate over who did more of the housework during the pandemic. You both felt like you did 100 percent of it. Things are no different in the workplace.

STEP 2: IDENTIFY WHAT EACH PERSON ACCOMPLISHED

Next, lay out what you think you each contributed. If the issue comes down to who did more work, be mindful of the amount of *invisible labor* that you each did. At home, invisible labor includes things such as taking out the trash, folding the laundry, and scheduling kids' doctor's appointments. At work, it includes cleaning up documents, checking and double-checking work for errors—boring but necessary tasks. Conscientious people do these things routinely, without being asked. Your credit stealer might be unaware of just how much invisible labor you've taken on recently (and vice versa).

If you think there's a mismatch in the amount of invisible labor you and your credit stealer have done, start with the following: "Lately I feel like I've done a lot of work. I did x, y, and z. Do you feel this way too? I think we should have a chat about all of the work we've been doing independently because there are probably tasks we are both doing that the other one isn't aware of."

The goal of these first two steps is to create a shared reality with your credit stealer. The next step is to think about what the two of you can do to prevent this from happening in the future. I'm often surprised at how reasonable jerks at work can be when they aren't personally involved in something. By taking yourselves out of the equation, you can work *with* your jerk at work instead of against them. In the following section, I cover some basic steps that should get you started.

Occasionally, you will encounter a credit stealer who, like Jose, is not motivated to find a solution to their credit-stealing problem. Unless there's a boss monitoring your credit stealer's every move (which there probably is not), I would distance yourself from this person at work. Avoid being on teams with them; don't accept their offer to "look over" your ongoing projects. Don't share advice.

If you need to explain to this person why you've distanced yourself, go with the "trust has eroded between us" approach. Avoid angry outbursts. Once you've made up your mind that you no longer want to work with this person, try not to get into a heated back-and-forth. Those conversations rarely do much other than raise your blood pressure.

HOW TO GIVE CREDIT FAIRLY IN GROUPS

So far, you've seen how credit stealers violate your trust in order to claim ownership over your hard-earned accomplishments; you've also learned how to combat them. But ensuring that credit is given when credit is due looks a little different when you're working in groups. Instead of a credit stealer trying to exploit your vulnerability, improper credit granting is often caused by a lack of clarity in group decision-making. In some cases, it's almost impossible to figure out where one person's contribution ends and another's begins. We also have some basic biases in human judgment that make us think our work is more visible than it is.

Before I go into how to prevent credit stealing in groups, let's look at where it is most likely to occur.

IN TEAMS FULL OF LIKE-MINDED PEOPLE

Diversity of thought, experience, and background in teams is important. Diverse teams come up with more creative and feasible ideas than teams made up of similar people. They are also less prone to mistakes. But there's another perk to diversity that people often overlook.

Because diversity of background breeds diversity of thought, people on diverse teams are less likely to come up with the exact same ideas.

I've been on a lot of teams made up of like-minded people. The first time I had an idea "stolen" while on one of these teams was early on in my graduate career. I told my friends about a new research idea at drinks on a Wednesday, and by Friday, my team-mate Jessica had already stolen it. Jessica wasn't even at drinks! I figured someone sold me out.

Jessica's betrayal was made clear about halfway through her practice presentation, when on slide 15 she laid out, in perfect detail, my study idea as her future direction. At the end of her presentation, she got a lot of constructive feedback from the rest of the team but not from me. My comments were thinly veiled accusations of idea theft, delivered in my mean-girl voice for maximum effect.

My advisor was not impressed with my behavior.

He called me into his office and there sat Jessica, arms crossed, refusing to make eye contact with me. Jessica claimed there was no theft—the research idea was clearly hers. Our boss told us to grow up and that the idea we both claimed ownership over was "the obvious next step. And not a very good one, at that."

Jessica and I had almost identical backgrounds. We'd both had the same research training, same skill set, same way of thinking. We had been reading the same papers and had an almost identical knowledge base. We had taken the same classes, and we had learned the same methods for conducting psychology studies. It's no wonder we both landed on the same idea within a seventy-two-hour window.

How can you avoid embarrassing yourself like I did? Changing the dynamic of my team wasn't an option, so to avoid this problem in the future, I learned to set myself apart. I developed skills no one else had and formed relationships with people outside my training background. Over time, my ideas got less incremental and more interesting and, most important, they never got "stolen" by a Jessica again.

And as I moved through my career, I reminded myself that when people work in the same space, they often come up with similar ideas. Recently I learned of a situation in academia where two sets of authors submitted the exact same analysis of the exact same data to the same journal, within days of each other. Crazy, right? I thought so.

The journal's solution to the problem was simple: have the authors from both projects come together to create a single project—one that captured all their expertise—and make sure everyone was given the credit they deserved. The authors could have accused one another of credit stealing but they didn't. It behooved them to find a way to work together, otherwise neither of them would get to publish the work.

IN GENERATIVE TEAMS WHERE IDEAS ARE "IN THE AIR"

Most people think that the best way to brainstorm as a team is to throw ideas into the air. One person comes up with an idea, the team tosses it around like a Frisbee on a nice summer day, and if it's good, they build on it. At the end of the day, the team creates something innovative and awesome.

Everyone wins, right?

Wrong. People get miffed when they don't get credit for their own contributions on teams like these, no matter how great the team's outcomes are.

Here's an example.

Imagine working on a team that designs dental chairs for patients who are afraid to go to the dentist (yes, this is a thing). It's forty-five minutes into the meeting and you've shared ten good ideas. No one's ideas are as good as yours. You know this because the head nods, smiles, and thumbs-ups keep coming.

At the five-minute wrap-up, your boss, Jason, says, "Thanks everyone for your awesome work! This was a real team effort."

What the hell, Jason? Why didn't you recognize *my* contributions?

Jason wasn't trying to ignore you—he was just not paying as much attention to you as you thought (or hoped) he was. You experienced the *spotlight effect*—a common bias that leads people to overestimate how much other people are paying attention to them. Have you ever fallen on your face on the street and remained embarrassed for a solid ten minutes afterward, even though no one who saw you fall was still around?

That's the spotlight effect.

When it comes to working on teams, we spend most of our time living in our own heads—we know when we say something smart, who defers to our expertise, and who ignores us—but we rarely grant this level of attention to other people.

In the same way, don't expect people to pay as much attention to you as you pay to yourself during teamwork. Like you, they are mostly focused on themselves. And when we are focused on ourselves, we aren't keeping tabs on other people's contributions.

The best way to prevent the spotlight effect from creeping its way into group work is to have one person keep a list of what ideas were generated and who came up with them as you go. Rotate the role of note taker so that everyone gets experience breaking this bias.

I like to start by creating a simple table that I share with everyone. One column says "Idea" and the other says "Whose was it?" At the end of a meeting, I have everyone spend a few minutes filling out each column. If there are disagreements, we handle them right away, before memories have faded.

IN TEAMS WHERE MOST OF THE WORK
IS DONE IN PRIVATE

For the past ten years, I've taught a course at NYU where students work in teams of four to create a single project. Everyone on the team gets the same grade.

Students hate this course. Mostly they complain about slackers.

So I came up with an idea. To make things feel fair, I started asking people to rate how much credit they should get for the final project, ranging from 0 percent (I freeloaded) to 100 percent (I did everything). I promised to incorporate these ratings into their final grades.

My strategy failed. Most people claimed to have done 80 percent of the work. No one reported doing less than 30 percent of the work, which is still 5 percentage points more than if each member contributed equally.

What is wrong with my students? Clearly, they overclaimed credit. But I don't think they're alone; most of us overestimate our causal roles. And when the work of others is hidden from view, we naturally assume we did more than everyone else.

Like a lot of work in teams, the majority of my students' work was done in private. Sure, they met once a week to go over what was finished and what still needed to be done, but most of their hours were spent alone at their computers in their dorm rooms. And like invisible labor, it's tough to know how much credit people should get for work that no one else sees them do.

To prevent this problem from happening, have people record

how much time they spend on each task they do privately. Not only will this simple step clear up uncertainties around who should get credit, but it will also uncover hidden roadblocks and bottlenecks that interfere with group progress. Sometimes a task is assigned to the wrong person; learning that Jack took three hours to do something that Josey could do in one will help the group become more efficient in the future.

HOW TO PREVENT CREDIT STEALING IN GROUPS

The biggest issue with giving individuals credit for teamwork is that you can rarely sort contributions into neat little "who did what" piles. But there are some steps you can take to add clarity to your team's process. The goal here is that at the end of the day, no one should leave the group feeling bitter and resentful that they weren't given the credit they deserve.

DECIDE WHAT EACH PERSON WILL DO BEFOREHAND

Before you start a group task, come up with a to-do list for each group member. The list should distribute the work evenly (if that's what you're going for), and everyone needs to agree on the list before you start. When the work is done, don't make my mistake and ask people to report how much they contributed to the final product. Instead, have each person rate themselves, and one another, on whether they did the work they *agreed* to do.

Credit is determined by the discrepancy between the two: what did you agree to do, and what did you actually do? If people know these questions are coming, not only will they be less likely to steal credit but they also will be less likely to slack off. You'll kill two birds with one stone.

TIE CREDIT TO WORK PUT IN, NOT SUCCESS OF THE OUTCOME

Most of us dole out credit after we see how successful a team product is. In most jobs, it's not wise to completely eliminate the relationship between quality of work and quality of reward. But when the *only* way to get rewarded is to work on the team that outperforms all other teams, you wind up with a hearty combination of credit overclaimers and bulldozers (more on that in chapter 3) who will do anything to ensure that their ideas are the ones that rise to the top.

Tie credit to the amount of work people put in, not just the success of the team's outcome.

I tried this strategy on a team comprised of high-achieving experts, all of whom expected to have a champagne fountain erected in their honor every time they said something mildly impactful. The desire to have "the chosen idea" impaired the group's performance. People spent more time jockeying for status than getting anything done. I switched things up and told them I didn't care whose idea they ultimately went with—I cared about how much work everyone did. It was a good lesson in humility. People had to put their noses to the grindstone if they wanted that end-of-quarter bonus.

ASK FOR REGULAR FEEDBACK

Nothing can kill team morale quicker than a boss who looks away from credit stealing. People need to feel like things are fair if they are going to stay motivated and engaged at work. And sometimes team members don't want to tell on one another for credit stealing, especially in teams with good chemistry.

I've come across a lot of these people, whom I refer to as "hesitant complainers." They love the generative energy of their teams, and they recognize how important it is for people to speak up and share their ideas. But after a big win, they feel slightly miffed. As one hesitant complainer, Jake, put it, "The last thing I want is for people to shoot down my ideas or steal them; I know how good I have it. But come on, everyone knows I did almost all the work here." I told Jake that when I spoke to his team members, they too each claimed to have done "almost all the work."

You might worry that if you raise this concern, you'll sound petty. And if you start and end with the complaint, you might. Instead, suggest to your boss that you have regular feedback sessions that will identify these problems early on.

If left untreated, complaints will fester into resentment, and before you know it, the positive energy of the team is gone. A few short meetings where group members can express concerns can make a world of difference.

EVEN THE MOST EXPERIENCED CREDIT GRANTERS MAKE MISTAKES

The science of granting credit to the right people is an imperfect one. Take, for example, the case of Frederick Banting and John Macleod, the two scientists who won the 1923 Nobel Prize in Medicine for the discovery of insulin.

Frederick Banting, a young orthopedic surgeon, approached John Macleod, the head of physiology at the University of Toronto, to ask for lab space to test out his hypotheses about how to extract insulin. Macleod, who was a big deal at the time, was not initially impressed with Banting's ideas; he found Banting ill prepared and unsophisticated in his thinking. But over time, Banting persuaded Macleod to help him out. Macleod gave him laboratory space, access to dogs (whose pancreases were used for the insulin experiments), and an introduction to Charles Herbert Best, an honors student at the university.

Macleod took off for the summer while Best helped Banting run several laboratory studies, periodically checking in on their progress. These studies set the stage for the eventual discovery of insulin treatment for humans with diabetes.

When Macleod returned in September, he was shocked at how much progress they'd made. He questioned the accuracy of their data. There was bitter fighting that lasted for years. Much work was done to refine the discoveries—largely by Banting and Best— but with important insights from Macleod.

Eventually, word got out about the work on insulin going on at the University of Toronto, and in November of 1922, August Krogh, a professor at the University of Copenhagen who had won the Nobel Prize in Medicine in 1920, visited the university to see what the excitement was about. Krogh's wife had diabetes, so he was motivated to learn more. Macleod hosted Krogh for two days, had him tour the lab, give a guest lecture, and even stay at his house. He also (reportedly) spent a lot of time convincing Krogh of his influence over Banting's work. Krogh left with permission to introduce insulin to Scandinavia. Shortly thereafter, he nominated Banting and Macleod for the Nobel Prize. They won.

When the Nobel Prize was announced, Banting was immediately pissed off. According to Banting's recall of events, Macleod's role was negligible. It was Best who deserved to share the award with him. Not one to hold back his feelings, Banting pointedly did not acknowledge Macleod during his victory-lap speeches. Banting had to be talked into accepting the award (largely by Canada, which was super proud of their first Nobel laureate). Macleod, who was famous for his refined tactics and ability to speak eloquently to the press, told people that it was "teamwork that did it."

Maybe Banting's response was justified. Decades later, Karolinska Institute endocrinologist and chairman of the Nobel selection committee Rolf Luft made a confession: the worst error the Nobel committee made was the 1923 award to Banting and Macleod for the discovery of insulin. The award should have gone to Banting and Best.

You don't want to wind up like Best, getting credit for your hard work forty-odd years after you did it (although to be fair, lots of places in Canada are named after Banting *and* Best). Instead, follow my guidelines for creating clarity in group processes. Develop strategies to make sure the right people are granted voice. Once you understand why some people are listened to and others are not, you can start building the skills you need to be heard. While you're at it, it might not hurt to learn a few strategies for connecting with powerful, influential people like Macleod did when he got August Krogh on his side.

Before you go

▶ Successful credit stealers are usually close colleagues. They are mentors, peers, and kiss up/kick downers on your teams.

▶ Like other jerks at work, credit stealers start off small and work their way up. They usually cover their tracks and steal only under conditions that give them plausible deniability.

▶ Credit stealers don't just overclaim credit, they sometimes underclaim it. By appearing humble and generous, they convince their bosses and new hires that they make great allies.

▶ Make sure the right people are granting you voice—they listen when you speak, and they remember what you say.

▶ The best way to gain voice is to form a lot of advice ties. Be the person the boss turns to for help solving tough workplace problems. And when you do contribute, be solution focused, not problem focused. Lastly, lift up the voices of others who struggle with being heard.

▶ When it comes to working in teams, it can be tough to determine who should get credit. In teams full of similar, like-minded people, it's not unusual for two people to come up with the same idea at the same time.

▶ Basic biases make it hard for us to accurately gauge our own contributions in teams. We think our work is more visible to others than it is, and we think we influence outcomes more than we do. These biases can lead us to assume we deserve more credit than other people.

▶ Having people correct their biases after they've determined how much credit people should get doesn't work. Instead, put steps in place that prevent credit overclaiming, such as having groups divvy up the work ahead of time. Evaluations should be based on whether people did the work they agreed to do.

▶ Tie rewards to work put in, not just the success of the outcome.

▶ Check in regularly with whoever is overseeing the team. If there are any cracks in the process, your boss or supervisor can act on them early.

3

The Bulldozer

ohn was a big deal—the operative word being "was." He was the first person at his company to ever receive a luxury car allowance, which irritated his coworkers. But who can fault him? He had excellent negotiation skills and exquisite taste in cars, so the allowance was put to good use.

John's first boss was Tom, a long timer whose gentle demeanor clashed with his thick build and baritone voice. People liked Tom. He had a lot of qualities in a leader that we often underestimate. Not only was he great at de-escalating conflicts between other people but he was also detail-oriented and for the most part followed the rules.

But Tom had a weakness.

He was pathologically averse to confrontation. If you came on strong and raised your voice even just a little, he would not tell you no to your face. He could handle conflicts between other people, but he hated it when people were mad at him.

From the moment John was hired, he identified and exploited Tom's weakness. John made dozens of inappropriate requests that Tom acquiesced to. He had a secretary file his taxes and a new intern make his family photo albums. Everyone else had to work hard for their bonuses, but not John. His bonuses were determined by the number of hours he spent in Tom's office wearing him down.

John's tactics were inappropriate, but they never crossed a line that human resources cared about. When he got frustrated, his voice would rise just a few decibels too high—not enough to qualify as yelling but enough to shake you up. He would stand about two inches too close to you—close enough where you could see the little broken capillaries on his nose and cheeks—and wave his finger at you like you were an unruly child. And it didn't take much to get him worked into a tizzy. Simply being told, "Sorry, John, your request is not a priority" was enough to set him off.

Tom hated these moments so much that he gave in to John's demands, no matter what they were. And in return, Tom got a happy and productive team player in John, who had skills no one else had. There was a reason John was given a fancy car allowance—he was five times more productive than the average team member. And despite his intolerance for being told no, he was in line to take over Tom's job once he left. Everyone else was either too inexperienced or too close to retirement to replace him. "All I have to do is keep John happy," Tom thought to himself, "and he will do great things for this group."

Then, to everyone's surprise, Tom retired five years earlier than expected.

At his retirement party, people expected him to announce John as his replacement. Instead, they got Susan, an outsider who hated secret handshakes and inside deals and whose experience saying no to the Johns of the world landed her the position. Rumor had it, senior leadership had gotten wind of John's bulldozing behaviors, so they'd conducted an outside search.

John tried to book a lunch with Susan to discuss their "mutual interests" her first week on the job, but she flat-out refused. The next week, he showed up at her office with a handwritten note from Tom, dated two years back. It read, "Upon my retirement, I hereby bequeath my office to John." Susan tried hard to contain her laughter but failed. "What the actual fuck," she thought. Clearly this relationship had gone in a very strange direction.

To John's horror, Susan treated him like she treated everyone else. She created procedures that made it impossible for John (or anyone) to bully their way into raises and better offices. She made sure that secretaries and interns weren't exploited by powerful people.

John did not like the sound of no, but he was getting nowhere with Susan. So he did what most bulldozers do when they're blocked from their goals at work: he took it out on his team.

John insisted on being on every hiring committee, and once there, he would refuse to support anyone whose "workplace philosophy" potentially conflicted with his. One person was deep-sixed because John had some argument with her in the comments section of her LinkedIn post three years earlier. Another because she reposted some article written by John's longtime nemesis.

"I can't believe she even had the guts to apply for this job after that transgression," John said.

Everyone looked at one another in disbelief. "I can't even remember what I repost online," one committee member said. "What does he do, spend all evening doing social media deep dives on these people?"

Yes, that is exactly what John did. And what he considered a social media transgression was not the type of thing anyone else cared about.

After about three months of this, John's group was exhausted and worn down. Votes ended in impasses because he refused to cooperate. Meetings were dominated by his long diatribes about respect and unfulfilled promises. Ill-equipped to handle John, the team broke down. Several employees turned in their two-week notices. The car allowance, it turned out, was not enough to make John happy if he couldn't also have his way.

MY WAY OR THE HIGHWAY

The story of John the bulldozer is not an unusual one. We've all encountered talented coworkers who are used to getting perks that the rest of us aren't privy to. Bulldozing is what happens when someone finally puts their foot down.

Most of us think bulldozers are people who talk too much. This can certainly be the case, but there's a lot more to them than that. Bulldozers are seasoned, well-connected employees who aren't afraid to flex their muscles to get what they want. Some held decision-making roles in the past and they're having a hard time letting go. In academia, we get a lot of these folks. They usually start their bulldozing with, "When I was chair of this department . . ." It doesn't matter if they were chair twenty years ago, they should get to tell the new chair what to do.

Others are newcomers who held power in their old jobs, and they assume that power should be transferred over to their new one. It doesn't matter that no one knows them here—they're a big deal and people need to recognize that.

And lastly, some have a set of highly valued skills, which they believe gives them the right to assert power over people in all sorts of decision-making contexts. A top salesperson might pull rank and try to take over decisions such as where the company will hold its next retreat, who's invited to dinner, or who should be named as the next CEO.

Bulldozers have two trademark moves. One, they take over the process of group decision-making; two, they render bosses powerless to stop them. Some bulldozers do this by threatening their bosses in private (as in, "If you don't give me what I want I will make your life a living hell for the next thirty years!"). Others threaten them in public. Like gorillas in the wild, they pound their chests and bare their teeth to show everyone who's really boss. And lastly, some simply wear their bosses down. People like Tom don't have the disposition to handle the Johns of the world, so they cave.

Bulldozers are the one type of jerk at work where what you see is what you get. Unlike kiss up/kick downers and credit stealers, they typically don't try to disguise their behavior. Impression management isn't a top concern of theirs—getting what they want is, by any means necessary.

For this reason, there tends to be consensus around who these people are in the workplace. Everyone knows that Larry interrupts too much, Candace wears the boss down, and Devon runs out the clock. Their private and public selves are consistent—those who bulldoze in one-on-one meetings also bulldoze in group conference calls and at company lunches.

Sneaky behaviors to watch out for

Like the kiss up/kick downer, they assert power early and often. Expect them to take over during the first five minutes when everyone is introducing themselves, or when the team is trying to come up with a plan.

They find teams that can't function without their expertise. A bulldozer is the only person who can work that new software everyone hates. They also know all the passwords.

They have friends in high places and aren't afraid to use them. Their kid plays baseball with the CEO's kid; they went to college with the head of HR. Most held positions of power in the past, and they have no problem using their old connections to get what they want.

They target weak bosses and bully them into submission. Bosses who are overworked, out of touch, and hate conflict make ideal targets.

THE BULLDOZER IN ACTION

When I told a friend that I was writing about how to spot a bulldozer at work, he laughed at me. "You can hear those people coming from miles away!" he said. "I think you can skip that section."

I disagree.

I used to think that bulldozers were the Tasmanian devils of the workplace—disrupting group processes and introducing unnecessary conflict—but now I think the proper analogy is the Trojan horse.

They sneak their way into groups by making themselves essential to the group's functioning, and then they take them out.

Most of us rationalize why we ignored the early warning signs. Sure, Larry talks too much—but he's the boss, isn't he supposed to? (No.) And Mina has lots of experience working in talent acquisition—why train someone else to use this new hiring software if she can do everything for us (and insists on doing it without any input from others)?

Sometimes it takes us months to realize that the people we've come to rely on are using our support to push their agenda. I've seen even the most effective leaders get taken over by bulldozers—realizing that with just five minutes left on the clock, those ten additional agenda items will have to wait. Best-case scenario, we sit back and watch our time being wasted. Worse case, we find ourselves having conflict over things we never used to fight about.

Bulldozers have a special way of turning people against one another. Sometimes they do this by planting seeds of doubt. "Do you *really* think Kelsey has the team's best interests at heart?" Other times they do it by creating coalitions ahead of meetings. If in a team of eleven people, five have already agreed to side with the bulldozer, the remaining five don't stand a chance. Unless they organized their own coalition, they'll have a hard time getting their voices heard.

In other words, bulldozers cause a lot of problems in organizations. Let's dive into them.

ON DAY ONE, THEY MAKE THE GROUP RELIANT ON THEM TO SURVIVE

When new groups form at work, the first thing they do is figure out the status hierarchy. Who should be listened to and allowed to make important decisions, and who should be ignored? Usually, power is based on skills or experience, but sometimes it is based on something else: who offers to do the thing no one else wants to do.

In chapter 1, I talk about the importance of establishing power early in groups—often within the first few minutes. Once the group sees you as someone worth listening to, you can persuade people to take your side and, eventually, take over group decisions. Kiss up/ kick downers use this tactic to get the bosses on their side. Bulldozers use it to go after a particular set of power roles—those that they identify as potentially making them invaluable to the group.

Truth be told, most of the time they don't have much competition. These roles include things such as learning a new software that no one cares about, agreeing to update the company website, or meeting with the not-so-popular head of human resources once a week. They don't *feel* like power roles, but they are. Without them, the group can't function. Let me illustrate with a story about Lora and her hiring problem.

"Three years in a row we've been running this job search, and we still haven't hired anyone. We haven't even managed to make an *offer* to anyone," she told me. "One more year of a failed search and the board will redirect the money for this position elsewhere."

Together, Lora and I picked apart the search process to figure out what was going wrong. Year after year, the applicant pool has been great, and Lora said they knew exactly what they were looking for. I asked her whom they put in charge, and she laughed. "Mike, of course! He's the only one who understands that program he created."

What program?

During the first year of the job search, Mike created a computer program that organized all the files, allowing people to sort applicants by different criteria, such as years of experience or highest degree. The head of talent acquisition had struggled to get such a program up and running for years, but Mike had coding skills, so he volunteered to do it.

Because Mike created the program, he ran the meetings. And because he ran the meetings, he controlled how much time the group spent talking about each candidate. "Mike totally takes over. We usually spend half the time talking about some person he likes who no one else is interested in," Lora said. Although he was never able to garner widespread support for his candidate, he was able to derail group discussions and waste a lot of people's time.

Mike didn't have a ton of social capital, and he wasn't on anyone's list of future leaders. But he had a unique skill that made him invaluable to the group. With that skill, he was able to gain (and enjoy) a little power and make the group dependent upon him to function. And from there, he was able to hijack group decisions.

The group was stuck between a rock and a hard place. Kick Mike out and add twenty hours to an already arduous process of reviewing files. Keep him on and risk being bulldozed.

THEY WEAKEN MANAGERS BY TURNING THEM AGAINST ONE ANOTHER

When most of us complain, we don't email the CEO. That would be crazy. Complaining about a problem to someone four levels up instead of trying to handle it locally is a quick way to lose the trust of your coworkers. But powerful bulldozers do this regularly, and here's why they get away with it.

Effective bulldozers are old-timers; they've belonged to the organization forever (or held a similar role in their old organization) and they know how the sausage is made. They know who the weak managers are and how to exploit past conflicts between managers to get what they want.

I saw this happen with Kyle, a bulldozer who used his knowledge from a prior life in leadership to kill a hire that his boss (and his team) was really excited about. Kyle's team was supported by Dale, a midlevel manager who had a decades-long conflict over something stupid with Miguel, the senior manager designated to sign off on the hire.

The original fight between Dale and Miguel was over an office space that they both coveted. (Potted plants were dumped over; mugs were thrown. It was dramatic.) But over the years, the fight evolved into a battle over job titles. Dale was bitter that Miguel held a higher position, and Miguel loved that Dale was bitter. At one point they dated the same woman. Miguel claimed he dated her first; Dale claimed he did. The two of them could not let their shit go.

Miguel's pettiness was easily exploitable, making him a prime target for Kyle the bulldozer.

"Listen, Miguel, as you know, Dale is in way over his head here. You *know* he makes terrible decisions under pressure—and left to his own devices, he will run this place into the ground. Can't you do something? We really need a strong leader like you right now."

Miguel fell for the flattery, killed the hire, and the conflict between him and Dale grew a little stronger. Kyle got his way, and the best part was, he didn't lose any social capital over it. He was able to exploit the ego of a senior-level manager to get what he wanted without anyone ever knowing.

If this sounds like something a kiss up/kick downer would do, you're right. Bulldozers got to where they are now because they were successful at kissing up and kicking down on their way to the top.

I HAVE A BULLDOZER AT WORK. NOW WHAT DO I DO?

Bulldozers are reactive. Once you start fighting back, it's pretty much a guarantee that you will be met with resistance. This doesn't make them particularly unique—a lot of jerks at work don't like it when people push back. But because bulldozers tend to be well-connected power players, there's a good chance they could work their connections and get their way anyway.

Does this mean you shouldn't fight the good fight? Absolutely not. But it does mean you should think carefully about which wars are worth waging. Before you get started, ask yourself, "Is this worth the fight?"

The answer to this question depends on one thing: whether your bulldozer is taking over short-term decisions that impact your day-to-day (meeting schedules, interview times, and where the company party should be) or long-term decisions that impact your future at the company (hiring decisions, raises and promotions, and how the new leadership training program will get rolled out).

Personally, I usually take on bulldozers whose behaviors only impact the big stuff. If you want to push back on bulldozers whose behaviors impact the day-to-day, be prepared to volunteer for some of their jobs yourself. Remember, they got to where they are be-cause they took on power roles early—and often ones that come with a heavy workload.

If you are willing to fight the good fight, read on. First, I offer in-the-moment solutions—things you can do right now to improve your chances of being heard. Second, I offer long-term solutions—things that require planning and preparation that will stop your bulldozer from successfully pushing their agenda behind the scenes. These two sets of solutions aren't mutually exclusive. Smart bulldozers get powerful people on their side before they bulldoze through a meeting.

I once overheard a bulldozer tell her boss, "If you stay quiet and let me do the talking, I'll be easier to deal with later." The threat worked, and the boss agreed to the deal.

Often, your biggest hurdle is getting those powerful people back on your side.

FIGHT BACK IN THE MOMENT

SPEAK UP EARLY AND HOLD THE FLOOR

During the pandemic, I developed a bad habit for dealing with bulldozers at work. All meetings were remote, so if I couldn't stand listening to someone, I would just turn the volume down when this person talked. At some point I started counting the number of minutes I put people on mute. One person (Stacey) spent four hours in blissful silence.

If only we could hit the mute button on people in real life.

But we can't. And when people ask me the question, "How can I get my bulldozer to stop talking?" I usually respond with, "A better question to ask is, 'How can I learn how to speak up and be heard?'"

Here's how to make sure you're heard in meetings, despite your bulldozer.

One, speak up early; don't wait for everyone to establish their voices before you. Bulldozers let everyone know where they stand within the first several minutes, and you should do the same (preferably with less grandiosity). If you're junior and new at this game, don't wait for your boss or someone else with power to call on you. Only the savviest of bosses know how to lift up the voices of junior people.

Two, if someone interrupts you, don't let them take the floor. In my research I've found that successful interruptions follow a pattern. If Person A is talking, Person B interrupts them, and Person B goes uninterrupted for ten seconds, then Person B won and gets to hold the floor. If you struggle to assert yourself, make a deal with your coworkers: one of you will intervene if another one of you is interrupted and can't get the floor back. The first time I heard someone say, "Can you please let Tessa finish?" I could have cried. I was young and in a fragile career stage and not ready to say, "Let me finish."

This goal can be especially challenging during the age of video conferencing. With everyone staring at one another in little boxes, we've lost our most important form of nonverbal communication: eye contact between two people. No longer can you say with your eyes and your body language, "Madeline, please, get this person to shut up!" And worse, your successful interrupter might be the *only* face people see. It is critical that if your meeting is conducted via video conference, you make the deal with your coworkers far in advance. Don't expect anyone to be reading your nonverbal signals when someone else is talking.

Three, when you do speak up, make it short and to the point. This advice goes against intuition—shouldn't you talk for longer? No, because we have a narrow window of time to capture and keep people's attention. I like to follow Marty Nemko's "Traffic Light Rule." You have thirty seconds to say something interesting, when your light is green. After thirty seconds the light turns yellow, and people start to zone out. If you're still talking at the one-minute mark when the light turns red, forget it. They've started fantasizing about their next vacation. Or in the age of video conferencing, started online shopping.

In chapter 2, I discuss how to gain voice at work in order to prevent credit stealers from seeing you as a target. That same advice also applies here. But it's important to make a distinction between gaining voice and speaking up: learning how to speak up involves in-the-moment strategies, whereas establishing voice takes time.

INFORM YOUR BOSS ABOUT THE BULLDOZER

When I told my friend Eric about my mute-button tactic, he was shocked. Not because I had done it, but because he didn't realize that he had lost four precious hours of his own time. I reminded him that despite talking a lot, our coworker Stacey made only a handful of actual points. It was just a lot of word-shaped air coming out of her mouth.

Eric's not alone. Most of us have a terrible memory for how much time people spend talking. We are good at remembering people's general points but not at how long they took to get there. Bulldozers love the outer monologue, especially powerful ones. In my research, we found that it takes high-power people about thirty seconds longer to get to the point than lower-power people; other research has confirmed this.

But no one remembers those thirty seconds.

What's the solution? I like to start with making sure my intuitions line up with reality. Download a talk time app and record the length of time people talk in meetings. If other people are worried about the bulldozer, have them do the same. Once you've collected enough evidence to document the problem, you can go to the boss.

And what are you supposed to say? This might sound counter-intuitive, but I like to use a loss frame in my approach. Let the boss know that you're concerned about how many people *aren't* getting a chance to speak up in meetings. Whose perspective are you missing out on by letting one person dominate the conversation? In chapter 2 on the credit stealer, I talk about the importance of diversity in perspectives in making smart group decisions. Highlight that point here.

USE THE BULLDOZER TO SOLVE THE PROBLEM

Once you've had enough, your temptation might be to tell your bulldozer that they talk too much. Surely the problem is that they have no inner monologue and they're completely unaware of how much oxygen they suck out of a room.

I wouldn't recommend this. Instead, try roping your bulldozer into helping with policy changes, focusing on things that everyone can do—including your bulldozer—to improve the chances that other people will get their voices heard (I go into detail what those policies should be below). Some bulldozers are truly clueless about how much time they take up; these folks can often be persuaded to use their skills to boost the contributions of others.

I once confronted a bulldozer who I was sure would hate being told he was talking too much. I approached him by expressing my concern that the junior people didn't feel comfortable speaking up in meetings. Then I asked him to use his skills to give a junior person a boost ("It would be great if when Steph is interrupted, you can stick up for her and make sure she has a chance to finish"). He was on board. Everyone likes to be included.

PROTECT YOURSELF IN THE LONG RUN

DON'T BECOME DEPENDENT UPON MIKE THE PROGRAMMER!

When you have a Mike on your team—someone with a special skill who can help the group make efficient decisions—it's tempting to hand over the reins and let them do all the hard work. And frankly, nine times out of ten I would do it.

But before you do, ask yourself a few questions. Does this person have a reputation for wearing down the boss to get what they want? Do they insist on holding meeting after meeting if the votes don't go their way? Do they interrupt people and manage to always hold the floor? If the answer to any of these questions is yes, then you should proceed with caution.

Lora and her team needed Mike's program; they weren't ready to throw out the baby with the bathwater. So instead of kicking Mike out, they created a training plan. Mike spent a few hours each week showing two newcomers how to use the program so when he rotated off the committee, the program didn't leave with him. At first, he had a hard time letting go, but in a matter of months he came around to the idea. It saved him a ton of time.

If your bulldozer refuses to share their knowledge, then remove them from their power role. Create roles that are rotating, so that no one person can control the fate of the group and no one person gets stuck doing all the grunt work. This might mean investing a little more time on the front end, but it will save you time later. Good processes have staying power.

Ten things to avoid giving a bulldozer

1. Passwords for company media accounts

2. Access to the company website for updating

3. Knowledge of how to work new software

4. Access to "protected" files, such as job applications

5. People's calendars or diaries

6. Code for computer programs, and for analyzing data

7. Access to company data

8. The boss's schedule—including when they pretend to be unavailable and when they are actually unavailable

9. Budgets

10. Feedback reports

LET THE GOSSIP TAKE CARE OF THE BULLDOZER

When John barked up the chain to complain about not getting Tom's office upon his retirement, the response was not what he expected. He hit a wall with Susan, so he tried her boss, Frank. Frank was a member of the original team who recruited John, and he was usually sympathetic to John's needs. But this time, something had changed. By the time John got around to asking Frank for help, he had lost a ton of social capital. Word of his petulance had made its way up the power ladder. It's one of the reasons why John wasn't hired to replace Tom.

"Instead of Tom's office, why you don't take an office in the new building," Frank told him. "Everyone thinks a little distance would do you good." John felt dejected, but from then on, he was a lot easier to work with.

Gossip is a powerful tool—one of the best policing mechanisms we have at work. For some, the threat alone that their reputation will be tarnished is enough to get them to cooperate. Your bulldozer might not care what you and your teammates think of them, but they probably care what the people in power think (at least the ones they haven't managed to exploit yet).

FORM AN ALLIANCE

A funny thing happens when a bulldozer goes too far—people start to become collectively angry.

Remember Kyle, the bulldozer who stirred up conflict between Miguel and Dale—the two managers with a long history of going at each other's throats? At the time, Kyle's team vastly underestimated how damaging his little power play was. For months, they couldn't get support for new hires. Unbeknownst to them, Dale was being blocked by Miguel at every turn.

After finally getting wind of what happened (someone overhead a private conversation in the men's bathroom), the group decided to approach Miguel and convince him that this decades-long war wasn't doing anyone any good.

"I don't think Dale is your enemy," they told Miguel. "Dale wants to grow our team, and we know that doing so is also in your best interest." For Miguel, showing that he could scale up a few projects was important for his pending promotion—he needed more employees on the books to reach his goal. "Why don't we work together to achieve *everyone's* goals," one group member said, trying her best to stay positive. It worked, and Miguel realized that spending his days on small acts of revenge wasn't really making him all that happy anyway.

Sometimes, the best solution for dealing with enemies at work is making new friends. Form an alliance with your team members and get on the same page regarding all the ways in which your bulldozer has been disruptive to the group. Stick to the facts. Once you have an alliance formed, you can go to the people who have control over your bulldozer's outcomes and make a case for why it's time to stop letting them get their way.

SET RULES EARLY

Larson was a clever man. For as long as anyone could remember, his team required a majority of people to be in favor of something for any new rule or decision to pass. But the majority rule was mostly an informal one; Larson's boss wasn't a fan of formalizing procedures unless he had to, so he never put this one in writing. But one day, a vote didn't turn out the way Larson wanted it to, so he contested it, demanding that the group reach a unanimous decision. Drawn to the scent of weakness, Larson's buddies formed a little gang of insurrectionists. What resulted was a massive infight between Team Larson and Team Everybody Else.

Don't allow a bulldozer to exploit weak procedures. Have clear guidelines for how the group will make decisions *before* the decision-making process begins, not during it. And if you struggle with a bulldozer who talks over people, include some etiquette rules as well, such as everyone gets a chance to speak before anyone gets a second turn. Larson took advantage of his team's lack of procedural clarity to start a war. But other bulldozers will use this an opportunity to "rescue" the team with their own set of rules. Sometimes teams are so desperate for clarity that they latch on to these rules, even though they don't serve the team's best interest.

When you make your rules, leave no stone unturned. Remember, norms about how people *should* behave are not the same thing as official policies. You might have a norm of using a majority vote because that's the way you've done it for ten years, but that's not the same thing as putting it in writing. If you realize a little late in the game that you didn't clarify procedures as much as you could have, that's okay. Take a small break from the decision-making process and address the issue now—it's not too late to add procedural clarity once you've already begun. Guidelines can be a work in progress.

DESIGNATE A TIMEKEEPER

Most of us have worked with someone who talks out of turn, interrupts others to bring up tangential information, and insists on introducing some new agenda item in the last five minutes of a meeting. Perhaps these people fail to pick up on the subtle cues—such as eye rolls and sighs—that it's time to let someone else speak. They certainly don't follow Marty Nemko's Traffic Light Rule.

If this sounds like your boss, they're probably misreading the room—mistaking the head nods and smiles for actual signs of interest. Unless someone steps in and interrupts them, the bulldozing will go on forever.

The simplest solution in this case is to have one person keep the group on track for getting through the agenda. If ten minutes have gone by and your boss is just getting started on that hour-long story of how he saved the day in 1975, then it's probably time to bring in a timekeeper. I've routinely served in this role for bosses who would free-associate all day if time permitted. People are grateful to have me there.

CONTROL THEIR SPOTLIGHT

If your bulldozer has no power and their behavior stems from a desire to be heard, you will need to take a different approach.

Think carefully about what drives your bulldozer. Are they desperate to feel relevant? If so, work with your team to give them a job that will scratch their itch to feel included. It doesn't have to be a particularly important job, but it does need to be one that will make them feel useful (I've seen this work with party planning jobs and a vegan lunch committee). Allot your bulldozer ten minutes at the beginning of meetings to update the group on their progress. By giving them time in the spotlight at the front end, they will be much easier to manage for the remaining fifty minutes.

I've lost days of my life—weeks if I'm honest—to bulldozers. I've seen them take over decisions ranging from what color to paint the walls to what the ten-year hiring plan will be. In almost all these cases, I should have seen the problem coming.

People often do nothing about bulldozers in the moment out of pluralistic ignorance—they assume that because no one else is trying to stop these people, the behavior must not be as irksome to others. The more likely explanation is that everyone hates having their time wasted and their voices snuffed out, but they just feel helpless to stop it.

Stopping a bulldozer requires short-term behaviors, such as speaking up and echoing the voices of others, and long-term ones, such as convincing the boss that they're being exploited and persuading your team to put rules in place. But the good news is, once you get a bit of practice, these behaviors will become well-learned habits. And you will get hours, sometimes weeks, of your life back.

Before you go

▶ Bulldozers are seasoned employees. They have experience, connections, and insider knowledge they can use to take over decision-making and render bosses powerless to stop them.

▶ If they don't have it already, the first thing bulldozers do is gain power. Some do this by asserting themselves very early on, others by bringing a unique skill that makes it difficult for the group to function without them.

▶ Once in power, bulldozers will climb the chain of command to get their way. Many will use their well-established relationships to trash-talk their teams.

▶ The first solution to being bulldozed is to learn how to speak up effectively at work. Assert yourself early, don't allow others to interrupt you and hold the floor, and make your points short (within the one-minute mark).

▶ Help others recognize bulldozing in meetings. Most of us don't have a good sense for how long people talk. Using a talk time app can get everyone on the same page.

▶ Put some steps in place so you don't become dependent upon a bulldozer to get a job done. Rotate service roles and set up training programs so the group is less reliant on any one person to be successful.

▶ Have clear guidelines for how the group will make decisions before you start working together. Bulldozers take advantage of loose procedures and rules that aren't on the books.

▶ Take control of your bulldozer's reputation. If you fear your bulldozer has gone over your head, form an alliance. The voice of a small group is more powerful than the voice of one.

▶ Some bulldozers don't have an agenda; they just want to feel heard. Find a job for these bulldozers—something that makes them feel useful—and allow them to brief the group at the beginning of meetings on their progress.

▶ If you feel like it's too late to stop a bulldozer, don't lose hope. Handling a bulldozer is a work in progress for many groups, and it's okay to go back to the drawing board and try different strategies as you move through the decision-making process.

4

The Free Rider

Max Ringelmann, a French professor of agricultural engineering, noticed a troubling pattern with his oxen. They had a hard time staying motivated when pulling loads alone—stopping to bask in the sun three or four times before making it across the field—so he put them on teams. Oxen, like people, he figured, could benefit from a little team spirit. But to his dismay, the opposite happened. The oxen didn't kick one another into gear, they made one another lazier. Three or four oxen worked at the same pace as a single ox working alone.

What about people? Surely human beings are more motivated to work hard than farm animals, right?

Asking himself these very questions, Ringelmann had twenty young men complete twenty-six back-to-back physical challenges, either alone or in teams, in one of the first-ever recorded psychology experiments. He found that like the oxen, the more men he put on a team, the less effort each man put in. In groups of eight, the men put in 50 percent of the effort they put in when working alone.

The Ringelmann effect, commonly known as *social loafing*, is one of the most tried and true phenomena in psychology (which is ironic, given that Ringelmann was not actually a psychologist). People decrease the amount of effort they put into a job the more people they have on their team. It happens in all industries, all cultures, and across all levels within an organization. If you work on a team, you will, at some point in your career, encounter the Ringelmann effect. It's at the heart of the free rider problem at work.

WHAT'S YOURS IS MINE

I've been in many groups that suffered from free riders. Even in retrospect, it is often hard to pinpoint why they got away with it.

I often assumed that free riders thrive because no one cares, or no one is paying attention. I believed that strong teams couldn't possibly fall victim to them. I was wrong. In fact, many of the same traits that make teams work well together *also* make them vulnerable to free riding. I call these the "Three C's": conscientiousness, cohesion, and collective rewarding. You aren't destined to have a free-riding problem if your group has one (or more) of the Three C's, but you are at risk.

Does this mean that you don't have to worry about free riders if you work alone? Nope. Lots of free riders target individuals. They are outsiders or newcomers, looking for a quick way to get ahead.

They target the most generous people at work, the bleeding hearts who feel guilty saying no. I call these free riders "time thieves."

For all types of free riders, prevention is about early detection and putting steps in place that signal to opportunistic free riders, "You won't get away with that shit here." It's also about setting boundaries, not only for your free rider but also for yourself.

The goal of this chapter is to give you the tools that you need to weed out free riding from your teams and to discourage opportunists from taking advantage of you when you work alone. But first, I'm going to dive into the environmental factors that create free riding in the first place.

Sneaky behaviors to watch out for

They take on work that has the veneer of importance but requires very little effort. Free riders are great at giving (other people's) presentations and emceeing the annual conference. What they aren't great at is doing the prep work that goes into these things.

They choose to work on teams where it's hard to sort out credit for individual contributions. Companies that dole out team bonuses, thrive on group competition, and don't care about individual accountability are their favorite homes.

They become superstars early on in their career, get overrewarded for it, and then sit on their asses. Fresh out of college with one esoteric skill, these folks have been paid big bucks just to not work for the competition.

Like the kiss up/kick downer, they are stellar teammates when the boss is watching, but they slack off the moment the boss step away. Having a team meeting with the boss today? Expect your free rider to have the most insightful ideas. After the meeting, expect them to come up with ten ways in which other people can execute these ideas.

THE THREE C'S: HOW A TEAM'S STRENGTH BREEDS FREE RIDING

CONSCIENTIOUSNESS

Conscientiousness is one of the biggest predictors of success at work, if not in life. Everyone wants to work with conscientious people. They are reliable, disciplined, and good at redirecting the group when people get distracted. And if you get a group of them together working on something they care about, they dominate.

They also make the perfect nesting spot for an opportunistic free rider.

Why? Conscientious team members almost always compensate for free riders instead of making them to do their fair share. Imagine a beehive that was just torn apart by a hungry bear. The go-getter bees, solely focused on the task at hand, will quickly get to repairing the hive, compensating for the lazy bees. In fact, they might even overcompensate, building a beehive that's stronger than the one they had before the bear came along.

The same thing happens at work. Imagine a team of five, with one free rider who does 0 percent of the work. To make up for that person, you would think that the other four (conscientious) people would each take an equal share of the free rider's 20 percent of work (about 5 percent per person). But strangely enough, they don't; they usually each do more than 5 percent. The group goes above and beyond what it would have done if they didn't have a free rider. For conscientious people who are afraid of failure, slackers are strong motivators.

One outcome of this process is that teams with free riders are rated more positively by their managers than teams without them. Because conscientious workers overcompensate for free riders, these teams actually do more work than the teams without them.

The savviest free rider I've encountered in my career was Derek, the man who managed to do almost zero work in two years. His team was full of stars.

Derek was a jack of all trades. He could write, be funny, and successfully manage large groups of people. His best skill, not surprisingly, was delegation. If there was someone perfect for a job, Derek would find them. He had three tricks up his sleeve: one, he made insightful, on-point comments that gave the veneer of contribution; two, he wrote carefully crafted emails detailing what work should be done but never made himself the subject of the doing; and three, he took on "work" that required charisma but no actual time (such as introductions and group presentations, written by someone else). Derek was always around, and he was well-liked. He did not fit the stereotype of a free rider.

Behind the scenes, Derek took advantage of his team's conscientiousness by outsourcing his work broadly and evenly across ten people, so no one felt weighed down by it. His behavior became problematic only when the company went through some layoffs and the team was downsized from ten to four. Around then people started noticing that Derek talked a lot about work but didn't do any. But it was two years until he was ultimately held accountable.

That's one hell of a free ride.

COHESION

Groups need cohesion to survive. Without it, interactions are fraught, painful, and rarely productive. At work, cohesion usually protects groups against free riders: the closer people feel to one another, the more motivated they are to work hard for the sake of the group.

But sometimes when we work well together, task goals give way to social goals—we slowly spend less time working and more time socializing. It's only natural that people who work well together will also want to play together. In fact, between 10 and 20 percent of us meet our romantic partners at work. But when you get along well with the people in your group, it's easy to let your guard down, allowing socially skilled free riders to rest comfortably on their laurels. We can also easily lose track of which team members are working hard and which ones are hardly working. Lastly, cohesion makes it hard to confront free riders. We don't like calling out the people we like.

I've had a handful of experiences working in teams where I look back and think, "Did that person do anything other than plan our social outings and gossip about our boss's love life?" The groups were successful, and at the time it felt like everyone was working hard. But if I think back carefully, only the conscientious among us were doing the work.

One free rider, Caroline, knew exactly how to exploit our team of friends. Caroline was well-liked and extremely organized, but only when it came to her social calendar. She got easily overwhelmed at work, crying over the most mundane things that "stressed her out." During crunch time she would get so emotionally dysregulated, it was easier to let her take a break and spend a few hours booking dinner reservations than to force her to help us (she was a foodie, so her talents felt well utilized). All in all, Caroline had a hard time juggling teamwork and her other work responsibilities.

We put pressure on her to help, but she always came with up what felt like valid excuses ("I'm so sorry I couldn't go to the virtual meeting yesterday, my internet connection kept going in and out" or "I'm so sorry, I had this other deadline last week. But it's over now, so I can concentrate on our work"). It was tough to get her to admit she had a problem.

Caroline reminds me of the free riders that were interviewed by Vasyl Taras—a professor at the University of North Carolina Greensboro's Bryan School of Business and Economics—and his colleagues. The authors identified seventy-seven free riders whose team members all said they did very little to no work on a team project. Even though each person was shown very strong evidence of their own free riding (such as multiple weekly complaints by all their team members), only 35.1 percent fully admitted to making no effort; 42.8 percent said the reports about them were not entirely true, and a full 22.1 percent denied them completely. It is hard to get free riders to own up to their behavior.

Like Caroline, Vasyl and his colleagues' free riders had decent excuses for their behavior. Many told the team that they were over-whelmed with other work; others had a hard time accessing what-ever communication tool the team was using.

You might expect these free riders to emerge out of groups with conflict, but that was not the case. In fact, only 7.8 percent of free riders in the study experienced any form of interpersonal conflict. Generally speaking, these teams were full of people who got along—were friends even.

COLLECTIVE REWARDING

In the last year or so, I've noticed a huge trend toward rewarding the collective at work. In fact, more than half of all public companies use some version of collective pay for performance (PFP), where people get paid based on how well their team did. Comparing individuals to one another, the logic goes, encourages Machiavellianism, reduces people's willingness to admit mistakes, and fuels jealousy and resentment. Rewarding the collective motivates people to work harder.

Some of this is true. Once people realize that despite working as a team only one of them will get the bonus, they tend to turn into the boys from *Lord of the Flies*. The worst version of this happens when companies leverage peer feedback—the ratings that team members give of one another—to single out one person to get an extra bonus or higher raise than everyone else. This strategy sabotages team dynamics. Rewarding the collective seems fair, especially if everyone contributed equally to the group's success.

But what happens when you can't tell who did what? You lose what social scientists call *evaluation potential*: the ability to sort out what each person contributed to a group's final product. Low evaluation potential is one of the strongest, most consistent predictors of social loafing—or free riding—in teams. Once people realize that their individual contributions aren't kept track of, they tend to slack off.

This might seem like an obvious point, but I've heard many bosses claim that individual contributions shouldn't be used to evaluate people if the team can't make it work as a whole. This is a dangerous move, especially if you have team members who lack intrinsic motivation or feel dispensable. It also makes your team vulnerable to credit stealers—the other jerk at work who takes advantage of ambiguity around people's contributions.

When I was in high school in the 1990s, I worked at a video rental store. One of my jobs was to manually rewind the VHS tapes (they were slapped with a "Be kind, rewind" sticker, but no one ever rewound). My shift of five teenagers was responsible for rewinding about two hundred tapes. At first, I was a conscientious team player. I rewound my share of the tapes. But about a month in I realized that our boss wasn't keeping track of anyone's work. Our bonuses were determined by how many videos the store as a whole rented out, not how quickly any one person turned the tapes around to get them back on the shelves. So instead of rewinding tapes, I sat around with everyone else and talked about who I wanted to go to prom with. There was no evaluation potential at the video store. And so we were not kind and we did not rewind.

It is not inherently bad to reward the collective, but it is bad to lose track of individual contributions. Teams that have one or two stars are especially susceptible to social loafing in this context; the free riders realize that the stars will carry the team across the victory line and they won't need to break a sweat. And with no one keeping track of their share of the workload, why should they have to?

Where collective rewarding is common

Most teams fall into one of two categories: those that do things (action or production teams) and those that make decisions (project teams). Collective rewarding is common in both. Here are some examples:

Product development teams: When teams are tasked with building something new

Sales teams: When the whole team must reach a benchmark before anyone gets rewarded

Production teams: When big teams are broken up into smaller teams, all of which need to work together to pull off something huge, such as making a movie

Hiring teams: Where the whole team needs to land a certain number of successful hires

WHEN THEY'VE WORKED HARD ENOUGH, IT'S TIME TO COAST

Silicon Valley has a little problem. To retain top talent, tech giants such as Google offer huge salaries to their best engineers to prevent them from working for competitors. The talent sits on their asses all day, and companies lose a lot of money retaining these people.

They call it the "rest and vest" culture.

As one engineer at Google put it, "What incentive do you have to work harder when you are already making five hundred thousand dollars in salary, and there is no more upward trajectory?"

New York University has the same problem. The university offers highly subsidized apartments to recruit faculty so they can compete with universities in cheaper parts of the United States. The catch is that come retirement, most faculty get kicked out of their apartments. Therefore, no one who lives in an NYU apartment has an incentive to retire, and with tenure comes job security. A coaster culture is created. Like in Silicon Valley, some individuals with huge salaries and fancy apartments are not incentivized to pull their weight.

What would drive a company to create such policies? Sometimes leaders fall in love with talented people. They think that pulling out all the stops to keep their favorite genius happy means that person will never lose their drive or run out of ideas. In other words, policies such as these are born from the idea that greatness will stay great. But unfortunately, all of us have slacker potential within us—even geniuses.

Overrewarding people for staying at a job without putting steps in place to keep them working is like giving your kid a candy bar *before* he's finished his homework. What incentive does he have to work once the chocolate is already in his belly?

THE ONLY WORK THAT MATTERS IS THE WORK THAT'S SEEN

Ohio State University Fisher College of Business professor Robert Lount and his colleagues stumbled upon a curious finding. Across different types of teams, high-status experts worked hard only when their team could see their contributions. If their work wasn't visible, they slacked off. This was even the case among teams that do high-stakes work, such as firefighters.

The reason was simple. People expect high-status people to be top performers; it's how they achieved high status to begin with. If they want to keep their status, they need to show up when it counts.

These findings carry an important lesson: We often assume that expert team members will always work hard no matter who is watching. It's the lower-status people we need to watch out for— the people who haven't yet proven themselves and who might be less committed to the organization. This assumption can lead to grave consequences. Just because a star teammate used to be intrinsically motivated to work hard doesn't mean he still is.

When Derek—the charismatic free rider who did nothing for two years—was hired, everyone assumed he would pull his weight because he did so at his old jobs. We didn't realize that Old Derek (the motivated guy) was replaced with New Derek (the opportunistic slacker). Seeing people for who we want them to be, rather than for who they are, is a common bias in psychology. Our group clearly fell victim to this bias, and it took us several years and a handful of layoffs to realize it.

Setting boundaries

1. If a free rider asks if you can help them pick up the slack but keep it "just between us," just say no! You won't get credit for work you're doing in secret.

2. If a free rider asks if they can get credit for all the hard work they did organizing social gatherings, just say no! These tasks are appreciated but they won't help your group make progress.

3. If a free rider insists that they are such a big deal and shouldn't have to "prove themselves" by doing more work, just say no! Everyone on your team needs to contribute, no matter how fancy their pedigree.

4. If a conscientious team member comes to you and says, "It's much easier if we just split up Jack's work among ourselves than try to force him to do it," just say no! Jack will learn that taking advantage of your team is easy, and he will surely do it again.

5. If your boss says to your team, "Don't worry about what you each contributed. I plan to split the bonus equally among you," (politely) say no! Free riders are drawn to teams that don't keep track of the work of each of their members.

CLEARING OUT THE FREE RIDER

Now that you know what makes your team vulnerable to free riders and what drives them, what can you do to prevent their behavior in the first place? In the following pages, I walk you through four steps you can take.

STEP 1: CONDUCT REGULAR FAIRNESS CHECKS

Fairness is a minimum requirement for curbing free riding at work. In groups, fairness applies to how jobs are decided (who does what), how rewards are determined, and how final decisions are made. When procedures aren't fair, people aren't set up to contribute evenly to the group and slacking spreads.

If you think you have a free rider in your group, do a two-part fairness check.

Part 1: At the beginning of a project, have the team make a list (together) of what each team member's tasks are for that time period. This insures task visibility.

Part 2: Periodically as you progress, have team members complete a short survey that checks on each person's progress. I use four questions:

1. Which items did you complete from your list?

2. Did you face any unexpected hurdles (for example, did some tasks take longer than anticipated)?

3. Did you do extra work you didn't plan for? If so, what was the extra work?

4. Did you notice anyone else on the team doing extra work? (This last question is especially important to ask in cohesive teams in which people might be hesitant to complain about stepping

in and helping a friend but are more likely to report if they notice someone else doing it.)

These four questions act as a "vitals check"—they allow you to test the health of the team and detect any warning signs of free-riding behavior. It's nice if your boss is on board with the fairness check, but you don't need them to be. Teams can do it on their own. I recommend rotating the role of vitals checker.

I often think about what Derek's team would have been like if they had conducted these fairness checks. Derek's list of jobs would be empty, and everyone else would have checked yes to "Did you do extra work you didn't plan for?" The truth is, doing Derek's work for him was a bad habit everyone had. And we know from research on habits that once a behavior becomes automatic, we no longer register it. It's like asking a smoker how many cigarettes she had that day. At the time she wasn't adding them up, but if she opens her pack, she can tell you, "It was ten, and I don't remember smoking half of them."

When it comes to bad habits, sunlight is the best medicine. If your group habitually supports free riders, the fairness check will tell you early enough in the process so you can address it (more on this later).

One last note for those of you who are a bit hesitant to suggest a fairness check: You might be concerned that others will label you a micromanager or, worse, someone who doesn't trust their team. This concern is common in organizations where the norm is to "figure things out as we go." Before you go forward, I recommend going to a handful of your team members, one-on-one, to propose the idea and get some feedback. Aim for folks who've been around for a while—ideally those who've been burned by a freeloader in the past and who would be open to changing the status quo. Ideally, you'll get a few people who are well respected within your group on your side.

There will always be people at work who resist change—especially if that change sheds light on their own problematic behavior. Your goal is to get enough support going into the meeting where you propose the fairness check so you don't get bulldozed by those who oppose it.

STEP 2: KEEP TRACK OF WHO HAS DONE WHAT, NO MATTER HOW CHAOTIC YOUR JOB IS

My two-part fairness check is straightforward if you have a job with very little uncertainty. But in some jobs, planning out your list of weekly tasks ahead of time is just unrealistic. Perhaps your job is fast paced with lots of last-minute changes, and you wake each day with very little idea of what will crop up. Maybe you put out (actual) fires for a living.

In these scenarios, instead of listing out each team member's tasks at the beginning of a project, have them document the work they've completed at the end of a chaotic day. Memories are fallible, especially during times of chaos, so fact-checks are important. I also recommend starting this process as soon as the group work starts. In Vasyl Taras's interviews with free riders, the majority of them admitted to free riding as soon as the work began (once they got past the denial stage).

Conscientious group members are particularly at risk for being exploited in these groups, and not just by free riders. Michigan State Broad College of Business professor Christy Zhou Koval and her colleagues at Duke University found that in high-stress jobs, responsible teams full of conscientious team members are assigned more work than other teams. Why? Because they show grace under pressure, and their bosses know they will get the job done.

These same bosses also vastly underestimate how much time the work takes to complete. Under high-stress conditions, slackers and stars wind up receiving equal credit for team successes.

I've been guilty of doing this to my team. I once ran an experiment at an industry conference that involved collecting saliva samples from CEOs and other executives, using a passive drool method (which is as attractive as it sounds). The goal was to measure attendees' cortisol levels as a proxy for stress.

Was this study a good idea? Of course not. Imagine trying to network at a conference and a research assistant walks up to you and says, "Please allow your spit to naturally flow into this clear tube." It was utterly chaotic.

My top performers were always within my line of sight during the conference; I spent the roughest six hours of my research career barking orders at them. The slackers were relaxing at the hotel Starbucks, out of sight and out of mind. By the end of the day, I was left with sixty tubes of spit and no memory of who had done what and when. I felt, firsthand, what Christy Zhou Koval and her team found in the lab. The better the conscientious workers on my team did under pressure, the more work I threw at them. And at the end of the day, I rewarded the team as a collective because I didn't keep track of individual contributions.

It's safe to assume that in stressful situations, your boss will behave like me: forget who did what to contribute to the team's success. As a boss, I was very appreciative when my team explained to me that a select few did the bulk of the heavy lifting during our saliva study. Sometimes bosses need help with fairness checks, and that's okay.

STEP 3: ENCOURAGE SOCIAL COMPARISONS

Common wisdom says that competition is detrimental to team performance, but research shows that the right kind of competition can go a long way toward preventing free-riding behavior in groups. When implemented correctly, a little bit of social comparison can light a fire under free riders. The trick is finding the right way to do it.

One common strategy for forcing social comparisons within teams is to tell employees that they will be measured and ranked by their performance. People tend to feel more responsible for their individual contributions, and therefore work harder, when they know how embarrassing it will be if they rank last.

But be careful not to make the final rankings public, like an evil college chemistry teacher who wants to scare people out of the major. You might think that the lower you rank, the harder you will work to improve your ranking in the future, but this is actually not the case.

Professor of economics at Purdue University David Gill and his colleagues found that after learning their rankings, people in first and last place worked the hardest. Top performers are averse to losing and get a high from winning, which drives their performance. Bottom performers are scared shitless that they will lose their jobs, which also drives their performance. But middle performers, who make up the majority of a group, reduced their efforts by more than 10 percent. It turns out, learning that you're perfectly average is demoralizing and demotivating.

This study is a good reminder that our intuitions sometimes go against what the science says. Telling people that their individual performance will be evaluated can be more effective than telling them *exactly* where they fall relative to others. Most of the time, simply knowing you will be compared with your peers is motivation enough to curb slacking.

STEP 4: REWARD THE PROCESS, NOT JUST THE OUTCOME

Animal researchers first observed an unusual but common behavior in rats in the 1960s. Rodents would press levers to get food even if they had a bowl of it sitting in their cages, simply because they enjoyed the process of working for the food. This is called *contrafreeloading*, and it is common throughout the entire animal kingdom; pigeons, giraffes, parrots, and monkeys all do it. (Cats don't contrafreeload—they won't press a lever to get food if a bowl of it is sitting right in front of them—but that hardly comes as a surprise to cat owners. Felines won't work for something if they don't have to.)

People do it too. At work, we often assume that the biggest driver of employee motivation is external rewards, like money. The reality is, employees will contrafreeload if they enjoy the process of their job. I saw this happen (periodically) in sales. Top sales folks would max out on the amount of commission they could make that month, but they would continue to push for big sales anyway. They simply liked the process of getting people to buy stuff. In fact, over-rewarding people with financial incentives can lead to *more* free riding, not less (as we see in Silicon Valley's "rest and vest" culture).

In other words, people are less likely to free-ride if they actually like what they do.

One of the easiest steps you can take to decrease free riding in teams is to give employees autonomy and say over how they work so that they enjoy showing up. You can do this by providing flexible work schedules (you can work ten to six or twelve to eight), not making income dependent on the number of hours worked but on getting the job done (people hate being forced to show up if there's nothing they should be doing), and asking for regular feedback on what creature comforts would make people enjoy their jobs more. Something as simple as an in-office espresso machine can perk people up. They tend to like saving five dollars a day on lattes.

Recognizing people's contributions as the group moves through its goals, rather than at the end of an accomplishment, can also keep up morale. Fairness checks will help you decide who should get those pats on the back. If the group is working on a small part of a big-picture project, keep them in the loop regarding how the other parts of the project are coming along. People can lose motivation when they don't see how their work contributes to something bigger and more interesting than what's in front of them.

And whatever you do, try not to let the work get too boring. Reduce the amount of rote work people do (people disengage when they're forced do the exact same thing, day in and day out), encourage them to change where they work (instead of sitting in a cubicle, work in common spaces or outside, if you have the space and weather permits), and mix up the medium of communication (Zoom fatigue is real; try meeting in person if you can).

Once with my own team, I lost sight of how little they cared about one of my pet projects. No one wanted to tell me, "Tessa, this research idea sucks. We don't want to work on it anymore," so they slowly started slacking off when I wasn't watching. I assumed people were intrinsically motivated to care, but they weren't. The study involved collecting data from one hundred participants, and for each participant, they had to follow a ton of steps. The minutiae of it really brought them down.

To help get the team back on track, I started creating a tiered incentive structure. Instead of rewarding everyone once the study was done, we had small rewards for hitting milestones (after every ten participants run in the lab, I brought in pizza—these rewards don't have to be big). I also took a close look at how people were divvying up responsibilities. To successfully run the study, five people at a time needed to work together. I initially based the tasks people did on their schedules, not on what aspects of the study they enjoyed being a part of, so I changed my approach. Some people loved putting physiological recording devices on people, so I assigned them that task. Others preferred being behind the scenes, watching the study unfold on camera and making sure the equipment worked properly.

At some point, people began to volunteer to help run participants in my study, despite having already completed their weekly hours. They started to truly enjoy what they were doing.

CONFRONTING THE TEAM FREE RIDER

As a kid, I was raised to believe in the Protestant work ethic. No, this isn't a religion; it's the general belief that hard work should be an important part of who you are and it's the only way get ahead in life. (For better or worse, our childhood experiences shape who we become.)

People like me have a very low tolerance for free riders. Our instinct is to punish them, preferably in some way that humiliates them publicly, so they don't do it again. But it turns out that public shaming usually works only for egregious acts (such as sexual harassment). In less extreme cases, people respond defensively, or they go numb and shut down completely.

Take, for example, the case of Chantelle and her teammate Drake. Chantelle learned of Drake's free-riding behavior about two months into working together, and she was pissed.

"Can you believe that Drake's been making his new intern do all his work?" Chantelle lamented to her best friend, Mina, in the hallway. "Lazy asshole. I hope he gets fired." Over the next few weeks, word of Drake's indolence spread far and wide. Chantelle had about a dozen conversations a day like the one she had with Mina, making sure to target the office's biggest gossips.

Did Drake change his behavior? Absolutely not. Once he learned of his new reputation, he disengaged from his team and did even *less* work than he was doing during his early free-riding days. The last thing Drake wanted to do was interact with the people who he thought hated him at work (nothing feels as awkward as walking into a room and realizing that before you got there, everyone was talking about you). Drake was *already* disengaged at work—which is why he freeloaded in the first place. The shaming put him over the edge.

So Mina's team tried a new approach. They enlisted the help of Heidi—the least intimidating yet bravest team member. Heidi had one of those faces that no matter how hard she tried, it couldn't look mean. To avoid making Drake feel ganged up on, they started by having Heidi meet with him alone.

"Drake, we need to have a little chat," Heidi said. "We know you have a lot to bring to this team. You have the most creative ideas, the clients love you, and clearly you're the best presenter. But lately we feel like you've been disengaged. Some of us are taking on some pretty heavy workloads." Heidi then gave Drake the opportunity to explain himself.

Not all freeloading is intentional—sometimes we freeload because we are overworked or micromanaged in other domains of our lives. The goal during this conversation is for you to figure out *how* your free rider will get over these roadblocks, not *whether* they will. In this case, Drake had no good excuses, but that didn't matter. Heidi raised the problem with him in a way that reduced the likelihood that he would respond defensively. The group then came up with a plan as a team to prevent it from happening again.

When confronting a free rider, don't expect them to own up to their behaviors, at least not initially. We know from Vasyl Taras and colleagues' interviews with free riders that most deny any wrongdoing. Instead, lead with a few of their strengths, including why you valued having them on the team the first place. When you bring up the issue of free riding, your coworker will probably be full of excuses, some of which might be quite convincing. It's critical that you don't walk away at this point, letting your free rider off the hook. Instead, work with them on a plan of what they will need to do and the timeline on which they will need to do it.

Only after you've tried to catch your fly with honey and failed should you move toward kicking your free rider to the curb. In chapter 1, I offer strategies for talking to the boss about a kiss up/kick downer who's making work difficult (in the section called "Approach Your Supervisor"). Much of that advice applies here. When you approach your boss, don't open with a character assassination (it will be tempting to call your free rider "lazy"). You have no idea where your boss stands with this person, and for all you know, your boss might be partly to blame. Maybe they put your free rider on nine other projects that they don't have time for. Start by opening with your free rider's strengths, followed by a description of their problematic behaviors. Then offer some suggestions for solutions. Busy bosses will be much more receptive to your complaints if you're solution focused and not just problem focused.

AND LASTLY, THE TIME THIEF

Not all free riders work in teams. They can also be coworkers, acquaintances, and friends of friends who try to wear you down and steal your time.

My husband, Jay, does a lot of favors for these free riders. I look at his calendar and it stresses me out. There's something called "lunch with start-up guy" on there. His best buddy from college has a friend who is in New York for the weekend and wants advice about his start-up ("It will only take an hour and I have to eat anyway," he tells me). There's a half-dozen twenty-minute phone calls with vague descriptors. One person is on there because he "might one day want to go to grad school" and needs advice; another wants to talk about his new podcast with zero listeners.

Suffice it to say, Jay has a time thief problem.

When you're successful and have a reputation for helping people, the freeloading requests are endless. Jay is the only person I know who responds to *every* request he gets. Part of his problem is one of pluralistic ignorance—he assumes that everyone at work is this responsive. The other part is that he's more giving than most people (it's not entirely his fault; he's Canadian).

I remind him that the majority of people at work are like me, socially aloof enough to give off "leave me alone" vibes. I also have thousands of unread emails full of random requests. Jay has none.

Jay's time thieves come from every walk of life. Some are co-workers too lazy to figure out how to do things on their own, so they bug him for help (many include fifty other people on their email request, but Jay's the only one who responds). These people are easy to deal with. Just send them an email with a description of how to use Google. Yes, it's snarky, but it gets the point across.

Others are go-getters who want advice or feedback on how to improve their status, so they reach out to every high-status person in their network. I don't blame them; many have been operating under the assumption that pressing the flesh is the first step toward making a name for themselves. Many are playing a numbers game, like the guy at a bar who hits on every single person he meets. Eventually he'll get lucky, and someone will say yes (that someone is always Jay—he wound up with a ninth grader in his research lab at NYU this way).

If you're spending too much time dealing with these free riders, put yourself on a diet. You're allowed to respond to a certain number of random requests a month—say five—and once you've hit your quota you're done. No more until next month.

The biggest hurdle you'll face in sticking to your diet is guilt. Who's going to help these people if it isn't you?

It turns out, lots of people. If you're like Jay, you probably know of up-and-comers who have something to gain by helping others—people who are looking to build their social network or want to become known as an expert. Connecting your time thief to one of these people will reduce your guilt and help someone else make a name for themself. You'll feel like you're helping multiple people at once.

After you've said no, don't get into a back-and-forth with your time thief. The smart ones are like telemarketers. They know that the longer they keep you on the phone, the better chance they have at getting money out of you.

If you work in an office, you might get a lot of time thieves who just drop in, without notice. Jay always had someone from off the street who "just stopped by." (I don't have this problem; I keep my door closed.) The first mistake he makes is inviting them in to take a seat. Once someone plants their ass on your office chair, it is very hard to get them to leave. I taught Jay to stand instead—preferably in some awkward space between his desk and the door—and have a very brief chat. The standing makes people uncomfortable, so they leave.

I've spent a lot of my life making excuses for free riders, and I'm sure you have too. Most are well-liked charismatic people who either have difficulty with time management or with handling the every-day stressors of work. Once you learn how to identify what makes your team vulnerable to free riders—some of which are surprising, given that they are usually considered strengths—you can put strategies in place to prevent it from happening in the first place.

Before you go

▶ Skilled free riders know how to infiltrate strong groups. How can you avoid being that group? Know what makes you vulnerable. I focus on the Three C's: conscientious team members, cohesion, and collective rewarding.

▶ Free riders are socially savvy. Beware of coworkers who slack off but aren't particularly disruptive and who have good reputations and social capital coming into the team. Often these people were known for churning out a ton of work at one point in their career but are now inclined to coast.

▶ High-status people are most likely to get away with free riding. Some feel like they've worked hard enough and they've earned the right to coast, others work hard only when people are watching.

▶ If you have a neglectful boss, free riding goes unpunished and becomes contagious. One of the main reasons why conscientiousness, cohesion, and rewarding the collective are problematic is because bosses aren't around to monitor team behavior. Without top-down oversight, skilled slackers can take advantage of strong teams.

▶ To solve free riding in teams, you need evaluation potential: the ability to sort out what each person has contributed to the group's final product. Once you've established this, fairness checks can detect early warning signs of free riding.

▶ Even if your group's work is tough to plan out in advance, keep track of each person's contribution as you progress through the day. Bosses easily lose track of who has done what, and they rely on team members to keep their biases in check.

▶ If free riding has become contagious, putting people in a competitive mind-set can help curb the problem. Learning that you will be rank ordered is often enough to do the trick. When people learn their *actual* ranks, however, only top and bottom performers feel more motivated to work hard.

▸ One of the simplest solutions to free riding is making people enjoy the process of work, not just the outcome. Autonomy over decisions, along with increasing group morale by rewarding small accomplishments along the way, can increase enjoyment.

▸ You might want to chastise your free rider for slacking off and letting the team down but try to resist the urge. Instead, focus on what strengths he has that the team really needs. People rarely want to engage with a group of people who hate them. Your goal is to coax them back into the team.

5

The Micromanager

ast week, I only made it to the bathroom twice without Karen
stopping me in the hall. The week before that, not even once.
I can't even drink coffee at work anymore! This isn't normal,
right?"

My friend Matt had a problem. A few months ago, he moved offices to a space down the hall from his boss, Karen. They used to be
on different floors, so Karen micromanaged Matt via email. Now it
just feels more natural to her to do it in person.

This didn't surprise me. If social psychology has taught us anything, it's that functional distance matters. We pay extra attention
to people who work ten feet to the left or right of us, not those who
work ten feet above or below.

Even micromanagers are too lazy to take the stairs.

Karen was a classic micromanager. She tried to control every aspect of Matt's daily work, from the way he pitched story ideas down to the signature in his email. She had a list of arbitrary pet peeves, which included exactly when he could call her (on the hour only) and the font he used in his writing. She was impatient and focused entirely on details, never on the big picture. If he said one small thing wrong in a meeting, she would email him three paragraphs correcting him. As a journalist, Matt worked more hours than anyone I knew, but he never seemed to get anything done. Everyone else who was hired at the same time had already been promoted once or twice; Matt had never been considered for promotion. The irony of the micromanager is that they work the hardest but accomplish the least. The same can be said for the people who work under them.

"What does it feel like, having Karen stop by all the time?" I asked.

"Working with Karen is lot like working with your toddler in the room," Matt said. "Just when you hit your stride, they interrupt you. 'Have you done that thing I asked you to do seven minutes ago? What about that thing I emailed you about three minutes ago?' The incessant questions fill you with a low-level frustration that over time really wears you down."

Karen was like a broken carbon monoxide detector stuck too high on the ceiling to reach. You think you'll get used to the beep, but you never do.

MISSING THE FOREST
FOR THE TREES

Micromanagers are the most common jerk at work. About 79 percent of people have been micromanaged at some point in their careers, 69 percent of whom have considered quitting over it. Eighty-nine percent of bosses think people quit because they want more money, but only 12 percent of people actually quit for this reason; most people quit because they don't like how they're managed. Sadly, most of us never confront our micromanagers, even when we have one foot out the door.

The micromanagers I've worked for were a lot like Karen: they disrespected my physical space and personal time, and they were capricious and unrealistic about expectations. Although I couldn't outright avoid them, I tried as much as I could to keep my door closed and to walk the long way to my office to avoid theirs. I memorized sounds of footsteps, so I knew which halls to avoid.

It wasn't until I became a manager myself and took a bird's-eye view of this dynamic that it struck me: Micromanagers are like icebergs. Above the water is the overbearing boss, but underneath lies the neglectful one. Micromanaging affects your day-to-day well-being, but neglect affects your whole career. Time is finite, and by spending so much of it micromanaging, these bosses neglect the important things, such as teaching people how to communicate, how to plan for the future, and how to make fast yet accurate decisions.

Take Matt, who missed all the big scoops. The world of journalism moves fast; he couldn't afford a boss who micromanaged font size and paragraph indentations. Karen didn't just miss the forest for the trees, she treated every tree like it was a bonsai—not a tiny branch out of place.

Matt could see the writing on the wall. If he stuck with Karen, he'd end up publishing little more than cat-up-a-tree stories for the rest of his career.

The next week, I took Matt and his coworker Khalil out for drinks.

"Last week, Karen disappeared completely," Matt said. "It's the oddest thing. I either hear from her ten times a day or not at all for two weeks." It reminded Matt of when he first started dating people he met on the internet—he could tell when he was in or out of someone's rotation based on whether they responded to his texts (which was either within thirty seconds or never).

"Must be nice to be ghosted," Khalil said, without the least bit of irony. "Matt, while you were enjoying your quiet time, Karen was in my office, loudly eating those chips she loves six inches from my head."

Most micromanagers don't have the bandwidth to micromanage everyone at once, so they put people in a rotation. They either have their foot on the gas going at you full speed or they've driven off to some remote location with no wi-fi service. Usually that location is the office of the person next to you.

Sneaky behaviors to watch out for

They ask you to do work, but it's never on a reasonable timeline. Everything is equally urgent, and everything must be done right now. Big projects (such as massive overhauls to proposals and budgets) and small projects (such as changing the color scheme of the boss's retirement party) are fair game.

They disappear completely just when you get used to the constant bombardment. Micromanagers don't have the bandwidth to micromanage everyone at the same time, so they rotate people. Expect one hundred emails or texts one day, zero emails and texts the next. And the disappearing act isn't a good thing—often it means you don't get the answers you need to move forward.

They assign mind-numbing useless tasks, just to keep you busy. Arranging boxes in the storage room, re-alphabetizing documents, and color-coding file drawers are all things micromanagers might ask you to do.

And if you are doing important work—a small but critical part of a big project—you'll never know it. Micromanagers are bad at communicating what the big picture is. Have you been working on a budget for weeks but have no idea what the money will be used for? Put together ten slides for what will ultimately be a hundred-slide presentation? These things are normal, but if you work with a micromanager, you will never see the whole thing come together.

WHY DO THEY DO IT?

The root causes of micromanagement are as varied as the managers themselves, but understanding a few common themes will help you deal with them.

THERE ARE TOO MANY REPORTING LAYERS

Fast, high-quality decision-making is much more common in organizations with fewer reporting layers—that is, those in which people have to go through only one person to get approval for something instead of three or four. If there are too many layers, managers don't have enough to keep them busy, so they turn to micromanagement. Especially for conscientious micromanagers (or those with a controlling streak), it's a better alternative than doing nothing.

I once worked in a coffee shop that had three types of managers—the shift manager (who did the weekly schedule), the assistant manager (who oversaw the weekly schedule), and the senior manager (who oversaw the overseeing of the weekly schedule). It was a small shop with not a lot of oversight needed. As a result, if I wanted to switch hours with someone, I had to get the approval of three people with little else to do. It was a nightmare.

THEY BELIEVE THAT MORE MONITORING EQUALS BETTER PERFORMANCE

Lots of people falsely believe that more monitoring leads to improved performance. If you hover over people for long enough, you will wear them down and force them to work harder, or better. It's what managers of assembly-line workers do.

Micromanagers are strong believers in this theory—what scientists call the *faith in supervision effect*. To illustrate it, Jeffrey Pfeffer at Stanford University Graduate School of Business and his colleagues ran a clever psychology experiment. Participants, acting as marketing managers, rated the quality of an advertisement for a watch that another person created. One group of people saw only the finished product, a second group oversaw the work but couldn't give any feedback, and a third group gave feedback that they believed was used to make the final ad. The kicker? Everyone saw the same ad. The only thing that differed between the three groups was how much involvement they thought they had in the product's creation.

What did they find? People in the third group thought the ad was much better than those in the first and second groups. They believed that the more involved they were, the better the ad turned out to be.

The problem with your micromanager is that they apply this logic to everything at work. Every single product—no matter how small—will be better with their relentless oversight.

THEY AREN'T TRAINED

Most managers are promoted because they're good at their old job, not because they are good at directing other people. And in the absence of actual training, they sometimes turn to "successful" managers for direction. Bill Gates, Jeff Bezos, Steve Jobs, and Elon Musk have all bragged about being micromanagers. We think that micromanagement shows dedication. And it might, but that level of dedication usually comes at a cost in efficiency.

Decisions that yield the most profit are both high quality *and* quickly made. Good managers can do both at once, but unfortunately this skill is rare. If your manager is lucky, they were trained on how to do one or the other, but probably not both at the same time. It's no wonder that in a survey of more than 1,200 employees, time spent on decision-making was unrelated to decision quality. Practice, it seems, does not make perfect. Only training does.

THEY HAVE SIMPLY RUN OUT OF THINGS FOR YOU TO DO

This explanation is an obvious one, but it's true. Not everyone is as busy as you are, with a hundred things on the back burner that you'll never get to. I learned this lesson during the pandemic. A handful of my coworkers seemed to invent stuff to keep themselves busy.

I remember the first time a micromanager assigned me pointless, mind-numbing tasks. I was young and working in retail. One day, hurricane-strength winds and rain kept the customers away, and no one in the store had anything to do. My boss, Ellen, couldn't stand the sight of us standing around, so she told my shift to go to the stockroom and rearrange all the clothing first by size, then color from lightest to darkest. From the moment the words left her mouth, I knew she was never going to check our work. And there was no rhyme or reason to the request, since we needed to find clothes only by size, not color.

Sadly, Ellen's intent wasn't to waste our time—she simply couldn't think of anything else for us to do. I later learned that on that fateful stormy day, some salespeople got together with one of the other managers for a fun, informal training session on how to upsell clients. ("Remember that awesome rain day when Stephen taught us all those tricks!" my friend Adam said a year or so later. "No," I told him with deadpan eyes. "That was the day I was arranging clothes by color.")

Years later, I found out that my team wasn't invited because Ellen was cut off from the in crowd at work. People show cross-situational consistency in how they behave; if you think your boss is irritating to work with, other people probably do too. And for that, we all paid the price.

THEY ARE DRIVEN BY FEAR

You'll be hard-pressed to find a micromanager who isn't afraid of something. A lot of them are afraid of losing power and status at work. Perhaps they're new on the job or they feel threatened by a rival. Others are terrified of failure; they were good at their old job (which was probably what landed them the promotion to manager), and they want to be good at their new one. Many feel like they're in a precarious position at work. One slipup from any member of their team, and they are out.

My manager, Ellen, turned into a micromanaging beast when a more qualified person, Joe, was hired to comanage with her. When Joe was on shift, Ellen would have me wipe down the counter every fifteen minutes (this was a clothing store, not a bakery). Like a hyena marking its territory, her behavior was performative. "These are my employees! They do what I say!"

Other micromanagers have a deep fear of making mistakes, either because of their own perfectionist tendencies or because there's a culture of perfectionism where you work. I feel for these managers. From their perspective, the best way to prevent mistakes from happening is to personally make sure that everyone who works for them dots their *i*'s and crosses their *t*'s. The irony of this approach, of course, is that by focusing on the little things, they wind up making the biggest mistake of all: neglecting the people (and projects) that matter the most.

WHAT CAN YOU DO ABOUT IT?

There's no shortage of advice out there on how to best confront a micromanager. "Take the time to clarify expectations and reassure your boss that she can trust you." "Convince your boss that in time you can do the work on your own." "Set boundaries."

I don't take issue with any of these pieces of advice, but they don't address the root of the problem. Micromanagement is not usually about a lack of trust at all; it's about other barriers that are getting in the way, such as the false belief that more monitoring leads to better performance, and that it's better to have people work on something pointless than on nothing at all. And the reality is, if the problem really was that your boss doesn't trust you, I doubt telling them "Hey, you can trust me" would solve the problem. This strategy doesn't work in romantic relationships, and I doubt it works in workplace relationships either.

To determine the best strategy to handle a micromanager at work, you must first ask yourself, "Does the work I do matter, or am I arranging clothes by color?"

Most of us have experience doing pointless grunt work at some point in our careers—my dad used to call this work "character building." But to advance in your career, you want to reduce the number of hours you spend doing menial tasks (unless you like them and have no plans of moving up, which is okay too) and increase the number of hours you spend strategically on projects that will move your career forward.

In order to do work that will help move you up the ladder, you need to look beyond your micromanager and interact with people outside your immediate circle. Find out how (or if) your work fits within the goals of the organization. I suggest finding some advice ties—people who know the ins and outs of the organization and who can help you see the big picture. In chapter 2 on the credit stealer, I provide guidance on how to do so.

I met an employee, Eric, who spent hours perfecting his weekly reports for his boss, who micromanaged the whole process. Eric put the reports in her mailbox and then moved on to the next thing. He assumed that his stellar work would eventually lead to a promotion. But two years into the job (and no promotion) later, he found out the fate of those reports: nearly all of them had been piled on his boss's desk, where they joined one hundred other never-opened reports. His hard work had become a fire hazard.

Sometimes, micromanagers are annoying to their bosses, so they're assigned useless tasks, which you then are made to do. I once asked a senior manager how he deals with micromanagers who work under him and he told me, "If I can't get rid of them, I invent committees for them to run. The work they do is irrelevant, but it gets them out of my hair." I immediately thought of people like me, stuck doing the grunt work for these useless committees.

If your micromanager boss is socially disconnected or, worse, has been sent on fool's errands by their own boss, then sticking around will harm your career. No one became CEO of a company doing fake committee work for ten years, no matter how good they were at it.

If, however, you decide that the tasks you're working on matter but you just hate your boss's working style, then I can help you persuade them to change their ways.

THE CONVERSATION WITH YOUR BOSS

At the heart of your jerk-at-work problem is control. Your boss has it, you want some back. There's a reason why bosses don't know their employees are unhappy with them: confronting someone who has control over your outcomes is daunting, so most people don't do it.

The good news is, control issues are so common in relationships, social scientists have put a lot of time and effort into figuring out how to talk about them in a productive way. We don't just quit jobs because our bosses are too controlling; we leave our spouses for the same reason. "Too much nagging" is one of the top three reasons why people get divorced.

In this section, I draw from the science of having difficult conversations to provide you with a guide to help you engage in a smooth and productive conversation with your micromanaging boss. Be prepared to try a few strategies that go against your gut instinct. If all goes well, you will both be happier with your new arrangement. Your boss might not realize it, but they will appreciate getting some of those hours back in their life too.

TIP 1: DON'T LEAD WITH MICROMANAGEMENT

You've probably been told not to beat around the bush when confronting your micromanager—honesty works best, even if it hurts. Matt tried this. He told Karen that she stopped by too often and it suffocated him. To help move the conversation along, he came prepared with solutions. He asked her to come by once a day instead of five times and give him at least three hours to get his piece written, not three minutes.

Karen scoffed at him and told him she knew how to do her job; if he was better at this, she wouldn't have to monitor him so closely. Matt shut down completely. He went back to his office, shut the door, and hid from Karen for the rest of the day.

Karen and Matt's interaction mirrors what relationship expert John Gottman calls the "Four Horsemen" of unhealthy conflict conversations: criticism, contempt, defensiveness, and stonewalling.

Conflict conversations that open with criticisms can quickly spiral out of control. Karen responded to Matt with contempt—she rolled her eyes, questioned his logic, and ridiculed him. To defend herself, she then engaged in reverse blame by telling Matt she wouldn't have to micromanage him if he was better at his job. Unhappy at how Karen responded to his criticism, Matt stonewalled her; he withdrew, shut down, and hid in his office.

TIP 2: HAVE A CONVERSATION ABOUT BIG-PICTURE GOALS

Instead, approach your boss and ask if you can have a conversation about big-picture goals. To bring down their defenses, I would start by asking a few questions: "I would love to get a better sense of how my work fits into the bigger picture here. What big jobs are you working on, and how does my work feed into these jobs?"

Because micromanagers are so focused on the here and now, they often forget to take a step back and remind people why the work they do matters. And like most of us, they have a *transparency bias* at work: they assume that the people who work for them know all kinds of things that they don't. If you've ever had a manager tell you to "make it happen" without telling you *how*, you've been on the receiving end of this bias.

I've certainly been guilty of holding a transparency bias myself. Research projects are massive undertakings—sometimes taking years to complete—and it's rarely the case that everyone involved knows how their work fits into the bigger picture. For instance, one particularly exhausting but necessary job is coding behavioral data. It takes a lot of hours for someone to watch an interaction and re-cord things like how many times someone sighed, or fidgeted, or nervously laughed when they were talking to someone else. For my students, having a professor look over their shoulder and say, "Why didn't you record that half-second sigh? What are you, sleeping?" feels unnecessary (plus it's rude). The first time I tried this approach I lost eleven people in a month. They honestly gave no fucks about how many times people sighed.

And why should they? I never explained why it mattered—I just assumed they all knew. The slightest deviations in our nonverbal behaviors can shape interactions in interesting and dramatic ways, but the data are useful only if they are extremely accurate. Once I told people this—and made it clear how important their work was and how it fit into the broader goals of the project—they felt much more incentivized to get those half-second sighs recorded properly. Plus, they were more engaged and less grumpy.

TIP 3: SET MUTUALLY AGREED-UPON EXPECTATIONS

Once you've established how your work fits within the team's lar-ger purpose, you can pivot to talking about the expectations. "What are the big things you need me to do, and what are the small, daily-level things?"

I've mediated a handful of conflict conversations between micromanaging bosses and employees, and one consistent theme has emerged: bosses often disagree with their employees on what work should be prioritized. Micromanagement is one tactic bosses use to try to get employees to realign priorities with them.

Matt and Karen eventually came around to a goals conversation, and when they did, one thing became clear: Karen thought Matt's job was to make progress on an article she wanted to see published, and Matt thought his job was to show independence and creativity in pursuing his own leads. They eventually came to a compromise. If Matt finished the work Karen prioritized early, then he could work on his own projects. When you ask your boss about their goals, it opens up an opportunity to bring up yours.

TIP 4: WHEN YOU DO CONFRONT, AVOID BROAD GENERALIZATIONS

After aligning your goals with your micromanager, make an action plan to move your relationship forward. But since micromanaging behaviors are roadblocks, you will first need to address the elephant in the room.

There's a science to confronting well. In Gottman's studies of how couples fight, he found two key tactics that marked a successful confrontation. One, no matter how frustrated one person felt, they didn't make sweeping generalizations about why their partner did what they did. Instead, they brought up specific problem behaviors without baking in an underlying assumption for their cause. Two, they sandwiched criticisms between compliments, which softened the blow.

In the same way, when you bring up your boss's behavior, don't just say, "You're an overbearing person with trust issues." Instead, stick to specific behaviors and how they make you feel. ("You send thirty emails an hour; it's a lot, and I find it hard to get my other tasks done.") Then, remind your boss not just what they can do less of, but also what they should do more of. ("But I really do appreciate the attention to detail you give to my writing"—whatever compliment you can muster.)

I reminded Matt that not everything Karen did sucked; she gave him very thoughtful feedback, and that's a good thing. Bringing this up helped ease some of the tension during their awkward conversation and it put a (temporary) smile on her face.

TIP 5: SCHEDULE REGULAR CHECK-INS

The last thing most of us want is to spend more time with our micromanagers. But all relationships take work. You wouldn't stop going on romantic dates with your spouse, would you? That would put you at risk of turning into roommates.

Like all other goals in life, the key to staying on track is having a system of accountability. Have short, frequent meetings with your boss where you update each other on your progress. Did we achieve our goals for that week or month? If not, what roadblocks did we face? Is the micromanagement creeping back in? If yes, you want to catch it early to avoid slipping into a demand-withdraw pattern with your boss: they demand behaviors out of you, you withdraw in an attempt to get them to leave you alone, and they respond by doubling down on the demands. This pattern is common in relationships—we do it with our spouses, our children, and, yes, our coworkers.

TIP 6: CREATE CLEAR BOUNDARIES AROUND WORK HOURS

One thing that has changed dramatically over the past few years is the flexible work schedule. People want to be able to work from anywhere, at any time. In fact, 51 percent of people would change jobs to have more flexibility. Millennials are willing to move anywhere in the world to get it.

Flexibility is great, but not if you have a micromanager. Micromanagers don't regulate their behavior very well, so they need concrete boundaries to do it for them. I recently heard of a micromanager who held her employees on an unscheduled conference call for three hours, well into the night. She had power over them, so they had to stay on and miss dinner.

If you work from home or in a different time zone from your manager, create some on-paper work hours. To start, plan your weekly or monthly meetings around an agreed-upon time that works for everyone. I have a friend in New York who works for a London-based company, so this means that most meetings with her boss are at eight a.m. New York time, not four p.m. New York time. Next, create clear expectations for turnaround times (emails sent will inevitably arrive in the middle of the night for someone). Micromanagers sometimes "forget" about details such as time zones, so these expectations can help prevent conflict later.

I also encourage the managers who are reading this to try to create some norms around work-life boundaries in their own organizations. I met a manager who included a simple message in her email autoreply that read: "I sometimes work at unusual hours, but I don't expect you to do the same. If I write you over the weekend, no need to respond until Monday." I liked this message. It very clearly signals "I am not going to micromanage you on Saturdays."

THE END-STAGE MICROMANAGER

Some micromanagers are wonderful to work with 90 percent of the time. They don't micromanage until right at the end, when the project they're overseeing is ready for prime time. They're the boss who won't sign off on a sale after everything has been checked three times, the editor who won't let you submit that journalism article despite having read it more than fifteen times.

My friend Trish had an end-stage micromanager boss. Patrick was wonderful to work with most of the time. But he was a bit intense. He once joked that he hadn't eaten a meal away from his work desk in fifteen years—but no one thought he was joking. His whole career, he had taken just two vacations. He didn't have much going on his life; no family, no pets to go home and walk. Trish was okay with the workaholic part because he let her explore her own ideas.

But Patrick had a small problem. Right when the two of them would be ready to move past the planning stage to the implementation stage on a project, he'd get cold feet. Perfectionism would set in, like a case of shingles that flares up only when you're really stressed. It didn't matter if they had worked on something for two weeks or two months, Patrick's response was always the same.

First, he would bring up small issues, then big issues, then existential issues. ("Does this work have any meaning? Why do we still work here?")

Patrick simply had a hard time letting go. He was an end-stage micromanager—focused on micro-indicators that the work wasn't good enough right when it was ready to go out into the world.

"Every time we finish planning something, he freaks out and questions my work," Trish lamented. "What am I doing wrong?" I reminded her that Patrick's problem had nothing to do with the quality of her work. He probably inflicted the same torture on himself.

What is someone like Trish supposed to do?

Trish was eventually able to get her projects up and running, but it took a lot of cajoling. I suggested that next time, the two of them come up with a plan of how to deal with his micromanagement *before* it set in.

"How about you sit down with Patrick and come up with a checklist at every stage of the project?" I told her. The thought of doing even *more* managing of her projects wasn't super appealing, but she was willing to listen.

I said, "If part of Patrick's anxiety is needing to check for mistakes, you can scratch this itch by doing it little by little as you go along, rather than all at the end."

Patrick and Trish made sure that the checklist included checking over each other's work—which created a system of accountability he was comfortable with. Both of them agreed, in advance, that if everything on the list was checked off, they could move forward to the next step. It was a bit like learning how to jump off a high dive. Each week, you try a diving board that's a little bit higher, until you work your way up to the highest one.

If you have a boss like Patrick, you'll probably need lots of these checklists. In addition to managing your boss's anxiety, they can be used to get the two of you on the same page regarding standards. The one time I was accused of perfectionism my response was, "I'm not a perfectionist, your work is just sloppy." Clearly, we differed in our definition of standards. The checklist made it crystal clear what those differences were.

As Trish moved through this process with Patrick, we had a conversation about trade-offs. Patrick had a lot of strengths, and Trish wanted to be trained by the best. For her, it was worth the occasional conflict to get that training. But we agreed that if her situation ever turned to one of learned helplessness—if she started to feel that no matter how hard she worked, Patrick would never be willing to sign off, and so she gave up trying—then she should leave. Work that never sees the light of day won't get you raises and promotions.

THE "MICROMANAGER" WHO CARES ABOUT DETAILS

A friend of mine recently complained that he made a handful of small mistakes at work, and now his boss was breathing down his neck. "I can't get anything done," he told me, echoing the familiar tone of the micromanaged. "She checks in on *everything* I do."

This conversation reminded me of an important lesson: bosses who pay special attention to micro-indicators—small details that signal that a much bigger problem is brewing—are not actually micromanagers. Unlike micromanagers, detail-oriented bosses are driven by a desire to contribute to the success of the group, not by the need to exert (arbitrary) control. Their detail focus serves a purpose.

Take, for example, Van Halen and the brown M&Ms. Buried in their lengthy performance contract was a statement that if a single brown M&M was found backstage, concert promoters would be forced to forfeit their earnings. Van Halen stage shows were elaborate productions that required a careful attention to detail and often hundreds of precisely executed steps. The M&Ms were used as a safety check. If brown M&Ms were found in the dressing rooms, what other, more important directions were being overlooked?

In some industries, such as the medical field, attention to small details is essential because the repercussions of making a mistake are great. A senior leader in the footwear industry recently told me that his secret to success was "attention to safety detail. It's the most important thing in the world." He learned this at his first job working as a busboy at a fast-food place. One day, one of the shift managers forgot to put up a caution sign after mopping the floor and someone slipped and fell. After helping the person up, the shift manager's boss fired him on the spot, in front of the customers.

"This probably seems like an extreme response, but *any* mistake related to people's safety must be dealt with swiftly and harshly, no matter how small the mistake is," the senior leader said. In some cases, little errors can lead to catastrophic outcomes; a good boss knows which mistakes are worth attending to.

If you're having a tough time distinguishing between a micromanager and a Van Halen–like boss, ask the people who've been working for your manager for a while. Experienced coworkers can usually tell the difference. In my lab at NYU, I have a fifty-point checklist for my psychology experiments. A lot of equipment is involved, and if any one item on the list is missed, the data we collect could be useless. The list feels like micromanagement to a newcomer but not to an old-timer, who will probably tell you, "Tessa cares a lot about this one thing (and obviously the behavioral coding—she's anal about that), but she's hands-off with lots of other stuff."

Paying attention to micro-indicators does not make you a micromanager, but people will see you as one. If you don't want your employees lamenting your torturous ways behind your back, have an explicit conversation about what aspects of the job require careful oversight and what aspects don't. Most employees are okay with some M&M sorting if they know they'll have other freedoms.

Micromanagers are one of the most misunderstood jerks at work. Most of us think they're out to ruin our lives, don't have a life of their own, or they simply don't trust us. But in reality, there's a lot of behind the scenes factors that lead bosses to micromanage. Many have popular beliefs about what makes a good manager (which are just plain wrong). Others are part of a system that encourages it, either because they aren't given enough people (or projects) to manage or because they fear punishment if anyone on their team fails.

Ironically, the best way to handle a micromanager is head-on, with more, not less, conversation. Learning how to build structure in your relationship will not only help get your micromanager off your back but will also give them some of their life back too.

Before you go

▶ Micromanagers are easy to recognize and label, but there's a lot going on under the surface. Ironically, micromanagers are also neglectful.

▶ Neglect comes in many forms. Sometimes micromanagers neglect people (they keep those they micromanage in a rotation) and sometimes they neglect important work. The problem isn't that they focus on details, it's that they focus on the *wrong* details.

▶ There are a lot of reasons why bosses micromanage. Most don't receive any training; they are promoted because they were good at their old job, not good at managing people. Consequently, they don't learn how to make quick, accurate decisions.

▶ Biased beliefs, such as the *faith in supervision effect*—believing that more oversight leads to better performance—also explains their behavior.

▶ In some cases, the root of micromanagement is fear. Fear of making mistakes and fear of losing status and power at work are two big ones.

▶ There are several warning signs that a workplace is micromanagement friendly. Ask the following questions during the interview process: What type of management training do people receive, and how many people does my boss report too? Too many reporting layers is a big red flag. If work schedules are flexible, ask how people set boundaries and respect one another's work and home time. Micromanagers need clear boundaries.

▶ The first step in confronting a micromanager is to find out the answer to the question, Does the work I do here matter? If you're arranging clothes by color, you might be better off leaving.

▶ When talking to your micromanager, don't open by criticizing them. They will respond with defensiveness, and you will respond by stonewalling. Instead, set up a meeting to talk about shared goals.

▶ When you do bring up their behaviors, be as specific as possible. Broad generalizations will only feel like an assault on your boss's personality.

▶ Even if it pains you, set up frequent, short check-in meetings. Healthy relationships take a lot of maintenance. Communication gets better with practice, so expect these meetings to get easier with time.

6

The Neglectful Boss

I used to underestimate how psychologically damaging a neglectful boss can be. Unlike other jerks at work, these jerks don't constantly hover over you or actively try to steal credit for your ideas. I assumed that the worse type of abuse at work is the kind that manifests in daily behaviors.

Then I met Kate.

Kate worked for Xander, a seasoned insider with a fondness for bespoke suits and cars he couldn't afford. Right from the get-go, Kate knew something was off. For the first two weeks, she had no idea what she was supposed to be working on. Other employees were given concrete tasks with timelines. But when Kate asked Xander for guidance, she was met with vague platitudes. ("Do what inspires you!") Kate found it frustrating, but her complaint is a common one. Failure to communicate expectations early on in a job is the number one complaint people have about their bosses.

"What about feedback meetings?" I asked. Kate quickly learned that scheduling them was a waste of time. Meetings with Xander were never based on meaningful milestones. Instead, they were based on how out of the loop Xander felt and how anxious he was to reassert his power.

On a good day, these meetings were short; Xander was distracted and disengaged, and he would wave Kate away after a quick de-brief. But on a bad day, the meetings felt like personal attacks. Xander was confused and combative, like a man who just woke up in a jail cell and had no idea how he got there. He would question why she did things ("Because you told me to") and then accuse her of ly-ing ("I would *never* ask you to do that!"). Then he would demand that she start over, or worse, abandon what she was doing to work on something else entirely. During these conversations, Xander seemed panicked, like someone was breathing down his neck to get answers.

The next twenty-four hours after a feedback meeting were an agonizing waiting period. Xander either followed up to make sure Kate was executing the unrealistic changes he demanded or he never brought them up again. The episode was followed by radio silence for a month or so. Then it would repeat.

From Kate's perspective, the worst part was the uncertainty and anxiety that constantly plagued her: "I can handle being ignored; I've always been good at figuring stuff out on my own. But I couldn't handle not knowing when he was going to show up and what he was going to say when he did."

Uncertainty is not a mental state that humans are well equipped to handle. For example, waiting to find out the results of a cancer screening can lead to levels of anxiety that far exceed the range of what clinical psychologists would consider normal. Experiencing periods of extreme uncertainty can lead to poor sleeping and eating habits, as well as persistent and intrusive thoughts. Most people have one or two experiences of daunting uncertainty in a lifetime, but for people with neglectful bosses like Xander, these experiences are frequent. The trauma that follows often carries over to future relationships. When Xander was eventually fired, feedback meetings with her new boss triggered a lot of anxiety in Kate—until she learned that her new boss was, thank goodness, nothing like her previous one.

OUT OF SIGHT, OUT OF MIND

I've been fielding a lot of questions from employees lately on how to get your boss to pay attention to you. "I ran into my boss at a coffee shop and she didn't know my name. Is this a red flag?" (Yes.) "I think my boss is ignoring me because she's busy having an affair. Should I confront her?" (No!)

Neglect is in the air these days. Bosses feel overworked and pulled in a million directions. Burnout is at the highest it's ever been among all employees, and it's particularly high among managers, who are often expected to juggle numerous tasks at once, often without clear expectations of what they should focus on most. One study found that 72 percent of managers felt more pressure to deliver during the pandemic than before it, despite having less time to get things done; more than half are currently experiencing routine burnout.

As a result, employees feel ignored and shoved to the sidelines.

Neglectful bosses are bad at managing their time and feel like they never have enough of it. Some follow mixed signals from their own bosses about whom or what to focus on. Like those who micromanage, one minute they're giving you too much attention, the next they're giving you none. Other bosses have a terrible time saying no to time thieves—those pesky favor-askers I write about in chapter 4—so they have none left over for you. But despite being the engine of their own time mismanagement, neglectful bosses really don't like being out of the loop. It's uncomfortable for them to show up to work and feel like they've just woken up from a coma—every face in the crowd is a new one and they have no idea why you moved the coffee machine.

Most neglectful bosses follow a three-step pattern: long periods of neglect, followed by a buildup of anxiety from being out of the loop, and then a surge of control to alleviate anxiety and get them back in the loop. It's a lot like a yo-yo dieter. Weeks of eating poorly are followed by guilt, then a three-day juice cleanse. The cleanse isn't a sustainable solution for the problem at hand, but it's a temporary fix to the dieter's sense of discomfort.

Good bosses, on the other hand, provide consistent and open communication, give people autonomy, and resist the urge to rush in, take over, and make rash in-the-moment decisions. Even when they are busy doing other things, they remain connected to their people.

In this chapter, I focus on neglect when it comes from someone who has control over your outcomes: your boss, manager, or supervisor. The experience of being neglected by a boss is particularly psychologically damaging—primarily because of the lack of control you feel—and so I focus on the strategies you can take to regain that sense of control. I note, however, that the strategies I talk about apply to any context in which neglect is happening at work.

Sneaky behaviors to watch out for

They ignore you for long periods of time, then sweep in and exert control over your work. Do you have a big presentation next week? Expect your boss to show up two hours before prime time, with one hundred suggested changes.

The control rarely happens when you want it, such as during the "ready to launch stage" when you could use careful oversight. Need a pair of eyes to look over your budget, read your proposal, or check your designs? Your neglectful boss is nowhere in sight.

The warning signs start early, such as during the interview stage, when these bosses overpromise how great your mentorship experience will be. They promise to meet weekly, check email hourly, and offer their cell for weekends if you really need it.

They say surprisingly nice things about you behind your back, often to create the impression that they are good mentors who know how to be star-makers. Expect your quarterly feedback to be glowing and full of superlatives— "major leadership potential" and "real go-getter!" These things sound nice, but they are rarely backed up with concrete examples of your behavior at work.

WHY DO THEY NEGLECT?

Neglectful bosses are on an endless quest for more time. Some of them have no time because they are too busy spending it on micromanaging someone else, others because their own managers take most of it for themselves. Whatever the reason, their behavior usually comes down to a problem of simply not having enough hours in the day for you.

THEY ARE TOO BUSY MICROMANAGING

The same underlying factors that cause micromanagement—poor time management, a lack of clear priorities, and a reluctance to give employees autonomy in decision-making—often also cause neglect. In some cases, the same employees who are neglected are also micromanaged. In others, micromanagement and neglect are directed at different employees. If your boss seems generally engaged at work, you might wonder what they are doing instead of paying attention to you.

In large companies, there's about one manager for every ten employees. If you haven't seen your boss in a while, there's a good chance they're' dealing with one of the other nine people on your team. And if they're a micromanager, it's probably going to be a while before you're put back into the rotation.

Although micromanagement and neglect often come from the same boss, the strategies you need to deal with the neglect side differ from those you need to deal with the micromanagement side.

THEY'RE CATERING TO THEIR OWN BOSS'S NEEDS

For every boss who neglects employees regularly and without consequence, there's a boss above them who lets it happen. If your boss isn't making time for you, it might be because they have no time for themself.

And it turns out most bosses fall into this category.

London Business School's Julian Birkinshaw and journalist Simon Caulkin found that the average manager spends 71 percent of their time doing things their boss assigns them: attending meetings, filling out reports, and answering calls. Only 29 percent of their time is spent on manager-driven activities of their choosing. These are things such as coaching, going over materials and giving feedback, and resolving conflict between people—in other words, the tasks that affect you most directly. In an average eight-hour workday, that's a little more than two hours a day of flex time. If you work for a large company and your manager oversees ten people, that's twelve minutes a day for each of you!

THEY AREN'T GIVEN THE RIGHT TOOLS FOR THE JOB

Imagine working for a cookie factory. The CEO holds a company-wide meeting where she announces her new vision: "From this moment on, we will be known for making the chewiest chocolate chip cookies in the world. And we will bake a million a day!" The CEO then turns to her right-hand woman, a C-suite executive with extensive experience in the baking industry, who responds with, "Great! Let's start by doubling the brown sugar in our recipe!" The

C-suite exec then turns to your boss, the floor manager, and says, "Now go make it happen."

In the modern workplace, most managers fall into one of three categories, ordered from the most to least senior: creators who come up with the vision, designers who bring the vision to life, and implementers who work on the ground to make it happen.

Most bosses are implementers. They are the floor managers who must find a way to make a million cookies a day. The problem is, most implementers aren't given the tools they need to do their jobs properly. Instead, they get "visual support" from the creators and the designers. They attend company-wide meetings where the CEO stands onstage and brags about their superior cookies. Then everyone cheers and shows support and eats the cookies. But what the implementer needs is concrete instruction: How many ovens will I have access to? How long does it take to mix the dough? What do I do if the brown sugar melts because the factory is a hundred degrees?

If your neglectful boss is an implementer and has no idea how to implement, then they will probably neglect. It's not entirely their fault—they just have no idea what to tell people when they show up for work.

THE DEVIL IS IN THE DETAILS, AND THEY DON'T KNOW ANY

It's only natural that, as you climb up the leadership ladder, you will know increasingly less about the day-to-day endeavors of your employees. Recently, I half joked to my students at NYU that if I got hit by a bus tomorrow, no one would notice. But if they got hit by a bus, my productivity would plummet. I haven't conducted on-the-ground research with psychology participants in years.

There are lots of good reasons why bosses lose touch and become neglectful. For starters, and as you've learned, the one resource they have in short supply is time. In their day-in-the-life-of-a-CEO study, *Harvard Business Review* (*HBR*) found that most CEOs work about sixty-two hours a week, and almost all their time is spent having face-to-face meetings with people to further their agenda. When it comes to executing their agendas, well, that's for the next person in line. The higher up you climb, the less time you spend on turning goals into actions.

I'll confess that I myself have been guilty of this neglectful boss behavior. I recently started a collaboration with a team of talented engineers at NYU. Excited about the work, I sent several emails a day asking them to do things for me. I thought my requests would take minutes to execute, but I was wrong, they often took hours. The truth is, I had no idea how much work went into computer programming. Only when a sleepy-eyed student confessed that he was up all night working on my whims did I finally understand. And yes, I should have just asked.

"THEY KNOW WHO THEIR STARS ARE AND LOVE THEM—BUT IT ENDS THERE."

This 2015 quote from Gallup CEO and chairman Jim Clifton highlights one critical flaw that many neglectful bosses have: they put most of their effort into their favorite people and leave the rest to fend for themselves. The CEOs in *HBR*'s day-in-the-life study spent a lot of time with direct reports but almost exclusively with the person(s) they trusted the most. Bosses have little time to spare; spending it with people who aren't furthering their agenda feels like time wasted. The outcome of this strategy is that the strong get stronger and the weak get weaker.

THEY ARE BEING EATEN ALIVE BY TIME THIEVES

In chapter 4, I introduce you to time thieves—free riders looking for advice to get ahead who target those who can't say no. If your boss has a revolving door of strangers and acquaintances looking for a quick way to further their career, then your boss probably has a time thief problem.

Bosses usually say yes to these people out of guilt. Lucky for you, guilt can also bring them back into the fold with you. A candid reminder that time is a zero-sum resource, and that you really wish they would spend some of it with *you*, often is enough to rein your boss back in. And to show that you're grateful, offer to take some work off their hands. You might even have something to gain by helping one of the time thieves, like forming a new connection.

WHEN BOSSES NEGLECT

You can come up against neglectful bosses at any point in your career, but there are four critical moments in which you are most likely to encounter them. Knowing these is the first step toward solving the problem. If you see a lot of red flags early in your relationship, you can exit sooner rather than later. And if you choose to stay, you can implement the strategies I detail below, like "need nudging," early, before the neglect has damaged your progress at work.

AT YOUR FIRST ENCOUNTER

About two thirds of people lie on first dates. About the same per-centage of people lie on their résumés to land job interviews. Bosses lie too—mostly about leadership opportunities that the job affords.

I remember my interview with Kila, the boss who promised to turn everyone into a star. Her speech at my interview reminded me of a makeover show: "No one knows who you are now, Tessa. But once I'm done with you, heads will turn when you walk into the room!" When I asked her for a list of people who were stars in the making, she shot me the stink eye and quickly shuffled me out of her office. Honest bosses have nothing to hide; Kila clearly did.

Why do neglectful bosses think they can get away with pretend-ing to be someone that they're not?

A lot of bosses think they can overcome their bad habits. We lead with our aspirational selves, not our real selves. Your boss might fully intend on being hands-on with you, but for reasons they might not even be aware of (described earlier), they struggle to get there.

In addition, by virtue of being absent, your boss probably doesn't know how bad their reputation is. They have no idea that when they leave the room, their team members will come and tell you, "If you want real mentorship don't work with Kila. She's never around." It's no easy feat figuring out what people think of you. Knowing office gossip requires lots of casual, daily conversations with people. And to do that, you need to show up to the office.

RIGHT BEFORE YOU'RE READY TO LAUNCH

Most employees value autonomy when it comes to making every-day decisions. But during the final stage of a project—the ready-to-launch stage—oversight from your boss can be critical.

Neglectful bosses have terrible timing. Those who err on the side of last-minute micromanagement show up when it's too late, and the rest never show up at all. Consider the case of the operating room. Right before a surgery is about to start, the whole team, directed by its leader, is supposed to follow a *time-out protocol*. The protocol involves a list of things that must be checked off before surgery can begin. If the leader responsible for conducting the time-out protocol doesn't do so, it just won't get done.

The consequences of ignoring the list are devastating. In fact, 25 percent of neurosurgeons have performed incisions on the wrong side of the head at some point in their career, presumably because a leader wasn't around to make sure the item "mark the RIGHT SIDE of the head" was checked off the list.

Most of us aren't performing brain surgery, but the lesson still holds. If your boss isn't around at the ready-to-launch stage, consider it a warning of potential catastrophes to come.

WHEN YOU'VE JUST BEEN PROMOTED

When we move up the ladder and acquire new responsibilities, we need training to help us get our bearings. But this is also the time when neglectful bosses tend to be more hands-off. Bosses often don't realize how critical it is to give people training during transitions in their career—say from floor manager to assistant manager. They don't see these as "new" jobs, just old jobs with more bells and whistles. In fact, in a survey of more than four hundred managers, the Ken Blanchard Companies found that most new managers are left with no training at all—a shocking 76 percent. In other words, neglectful bosses aren't born, they are made. And if yours is a neglectful one, expect them to pass on the gene.

There's another reason why your boss doesn't help you during your transition that might come as a surprise: they might be trying to show respect, not neglect. A friend of mine was recently promoted to a C-suite position, and the CEO gave her very little hands-on instruction. She felt lost, like he hired her and forgot about her. But when she expressed concern, he was surprised. His goal was to show her that he trusted her to make her own decisions.

Your boss could be operating under the misconception that following your promotion, you prefer to handle things on your own. Good bosses don't want to overstep their bounds after promoting people; finding your voice is important for establishing yourself in the hierarchy at work. If this is the case, clear communication can go a long way.

WHEN IT'S TIME TO GET EVALUATED

When the time comes for their own performance evaluations, neglectful bosses realize just how little they know about what's going on with their team. So they go to extremes to make up for it, sometimes conducting hours-long check-ins with you to catch up on everything they've missed.

I once knew a boss, Christie, who grilled her employees the night before she met with her boss to find out what they'd been up to for the past four months. They found it jarring; four months of almost no communication and now a three-hour grill session? Why would

Christie do this? Because she knew that part of what made her look like a strong team leader was keeping track of the progress of her employees. She wanted to give off the impression that she was "on top of things"—she knew exactly what her employees had and hadn't done and who the rising stars were. The strategy was an impression-management technique. Neglectful bosses know how important good mentorship is, so they need to at least pretend to be good at it when you aren't around.

I HAVE A NEGLECTFUL BOSS. NOW WHAT SHOULD I DO?

To get your neglectful boss back on track, you first need to identify the specific issue that's contributing to their behavior. In some cases, it's miscommunication; your boss doesn't realize that you want more hands-on attention than you're getting. In others, your boss is burned out and overwhelmed, and you can play an active role in helping them re-engage with you. Once you know what you're up against, tailor the following techniques to your situation.

NEED-NUDGE

Like all relationships that involve communication difficulties, it's important to ask yourself, How much of the neglect could be reduced if I simply clearly communicated my needs?

Neglectful bosses with poor time-management skills and those who are pulled in a million directions might be so focused on their needs that they forget about yours. And if you've recently taken on new responsibilities at work, your boss might think you're so competent you don't need more guidance.

Need-nudging is a strategy of carefully conveying to your boss "I need more of your time." It's not declaring an emergency or coming to your boss with a list of fifteen things you need help with right now. Need-nudging is subtle. It's about finding the appropriate ask within the appropriate time frame, given all of your boss's other responsibilities.

When you need-nudge, be concrete about what you need help with and give a window of time in which that help can be given. Write a short email (five lines or fewer according to my busiest boss friends) and ask for a thirty-minute meeting if you can (lots of bosses operate in thirty-minute windows, not one-hour ones). Most of us think that if we act like it's an emergency, our boss is more likely to respond, but this is not usually the case. They are less likely to respond. The chance that they can fit you into their busy schedule in the next forty-eight hours is slim. They are more likely to be able to fit you in over the next two weeks.

When I was writing this book, I became the boss who had to be need-nudged. (It turns out it was hard to write a book and keep up with my job as a professor at the same time. Who would have thought!) I bit off more than I could chew—something most of you can probably relate to.

When I was under a tight book deadline, I became hard to reach. The only thing I could think about was writing—everything else, including documents that needed signing, papers that needed grading, and projects that needed to be evaluated, went on the back burner.

It took about a year to write this book, so clearly this strategy of going in and out of ghosting my students was not sustainable.

When my team first realized what was happening, they panicked. Their intuition was to beg for a meeting out of desperation. "Squeeze me in whenever. Weekends, nine p.m., it doesn't matter. I just need thirty minutes." This strategy did not work—I didn't *want* to squeeze them in at odd hours. I felt overworked and overwhelmed.

Besides, that's no way for them to live.

Over time, we realized that half of my stress about these meetings stemmed from the relentless back-and-forth over schedules (for anyone who has filled out their availability on one of those calendar apps, you know what I mean). To solve the problem, I created a monthly calendar on Google Drive that only the five members of my lab at NYU had access to, along with my lab manager, who in most workplaces is your boss's secretary or personal assistant. I added hours of availability—blocking off everything else—and I shared the link with the select group of people who were at risk of being neglected.

No more back-and-forth, no more trying to squeeze people into weird times. People could sign up for this week (if I happened to have a window or two available) or next month. The organized people signed up for multiple meetings at once to lock in their preferred times.

The calendar method can reduce a lot of stress that neglectful bosses, like me, feel when they realize they're letting important things go at work. It takes the guesswork out of who wants more face time and who prefers touching base once a month. It also gives everyone an equal opportunity to meet with the boss; prioritization isn't given to the people who feel more comfortable hounding them. I no longer had to worry about the newcomer who *might* want more time with me but was too shy to say so.

Once at the meetings, my students got very good at controlling the agenda and monitoring the time. If there were three important items to cover in those thirty minutes, they made sure to stay on task and spend ten minutes on each one. As an overworked boss, I didn't mind handing over the reins to someone else. I bet your boss won't either.

How can you get your neglectful boss to follow my lead? I was hesitant at first—the last thing I needed was another calendar in my life. Therefore, it's important to remind your boss that this isn't a calendar for everyone—it's only for those with whom they work closely who are feeling a little ignored these days. Use it for scheduling group meetings that can't happen unless your neglectful boss is available. If your boss is anything like me, they will be happy not to have to fill out another one of those availability apps with sixty specified times spanning the next six weeks. They will log in and see that you've already done the hard work for them and found a time that works for everyone, including them.

If you practice need-nudging regularly, your boss will soon realize that setting small amounts of time aside to help you now will save her a ton of time later.

Julian Birkinshaw and Simon Caulkin found that when bosses rearranged their calendars for the first three weeks out of the year to spend an extra two hours a day with their teams, they saw massive improvements in performance. The key was that those two hours a day were spent with teams at the beginning of the year, before big projects were underway, not during the year. By getting hands-on help early, team members became more independent and less needy during crunch time. They also learned how to turn to one another as a resource.

ASK FOR LESS AND TAKE ON MORE

If the neglect feels temporary—your boss is usually great about feedback but recently has started to let things slide—there might be a situational explanation for it, like a global pandemic, for instance. Ironically, one of the best things you can do to help a neglectful boss in situations like these is to offer up things they *can* neglect.

Think about it this way. Imagine walking into your kitchen and seeing a big mess. There are fifty dishes in the sink and a broken trash bag with yesterday's dinner spilled on the floor. You wouldn't want to clean any of it, right?

When we're overwhelmed with the amount of work in front of us, our tendency isn't to chip away at it, it's to disengage from all of it. Your boss might have more work than they can handle. And once burnout sets in, don't expect much hands-on mentoring.

I remember the first time I witnessed an involved boss—Dylan—turn into an outright neglecter. Dylan was the best mentor I knew; he would spend hours with his direct reports giving them useful feedback, teaching them everything from how to approach a power player at a conference to how to handle negative feedback from team members. He was like a gardener with his orchids—spraying them with water twice a day and making sure that they had the exact hours of sunshine they needed to thrive.

Then one day, Dylan got a promotion. Because he was so good at mentoring, his boss expanded his team from five to ten. What Dylan and his boss didn't realize was that Dylan's method of mentoring did not scale—not even to five more people. His sweet spot was a team of four or five. Any bigger than that and the whole house came crashing down.

At first, Dylan tried. He spent sixty hours a week at work instead of forty, trying to squeeze everyone in. But a few months later, he crashed and burned. Because he couldn't give everyone four hours a week of his time, he gave nobody four hours a week of his time, or even one hour. He didn't feel comfortable playing favorites and he didn't know how to change his approach.

If you have a boss like Dylan, the onus might fall on you to help them learn a new way of mentoring. Take a break from asking for more face time or feedback and instead offer to off-load some of that work. One simple way to do this is by creating a priority list. Make it clear to your boss that among the ten things you need help with, nine can wait. Simply being told that nine things can wait might be enough to reduce your boss's stress, get them to re-engage with you, and reduce your stress about being neglected.

You can also offer to take on some of your boss's work for them. I know, most of you are probably thinking, "I have a neglectful boss and you think the solution is to do their work for them? That hardly seems fair."

Hear me out.

Your boss has a finite amount of time, and you want some of it. To get it, you will need to take it away from something else they are doing. If you choose wisely, you might get a lot more time back than you expect. Some of the tasks your boss is doing, quite frankly, you probably could do more quickly than they can. These tasks include things such as writing the first draft of a weekly newsletter that your boss is in charge of sending, responding to routine emails, and digging up information online about some topic. Because your boss is probably multitasking when they do these things (which we know from research is the worst thing we can do with our time—it's quite impossible to concentrate on two things at once), they probably take twice as long as you would to do them. If you're more efficient at these tasks than your boss, you might lose one hour but they gain three. Just make sure at least one of those three hours is reserved for you.

SUPPLEMENT YOUR BOSS WITH OTHER EXPERTS

These days, we expect a wide range of expertise from our bosses, from guidance on planning our next big career move, to advice on how to give a solid presentation, to technical knowledge on how to operate a new system at work. Neglectful bosses might be burned out or short on time and therefore unable to help in a meaningful way. When this happens, don't be afraid to call on other people to fill in the gaps. Sometimes that other person is a former employee. ("Why don't you ask Simone to go over the new communications system with you; she's an expert.") Other times it's a coworker who you know isn't as overwhelmed as your boss.

The people who've been working for me for a while know how to ask around for help when I'm short on time, but I've noticed a pattern with new employees. Almost none of them do it of their own voli- tion. Why? They often think I will be offended that they went outside of the relationship to get mentored. "I was afraid you would think I was going behind your back to get help," one person told me. I laughed at this. "I love it when people go behind my back to get help!"

Bosses can be territorial. But the reality is, most are grateful when their employees find other people to turn to for help. And if you aren't sure, ask. "I notice you've been swamped lately. Is it okay if I set up a time with Simone to go over the new communications system?"

Other bosses neglect because they just don't have expertise (and they're too ashamed to admit it). If that's the case with your neglect-ful boss, then learning how to supplement that expertise with help from others will be especially critical for your career. In chapter 2, I talk about the importance of learning how to find advice ties at work—people who know how to get shit done. Those same advice ties are critical for helping you get ahead at work when your boss isn't around.

HELP YOUR BOSS REALIZE
THEY'RE NEGLECTFUL

Out of all the jerks at work, neglectful bosses are the least self-aware. Some are in flat-out denial; they used to be hands-on bosses but for reasons I've outlined above, they've let things go. Others, like Xander, are so out of the loop, they don't know how much they deviate from the norm, and they don't stick around long enough to see how other bosses behave at work.

Even when I could feel myself being neglectful, no one flat-out told me, "Tessa, you suck as a mentor right now. We miss Old Tessa." I learned I was neglecting them based on the desperate looks on their faces.

Don't expect your boss to figure out how miserable you are. In-stead, come to them with a plan—including how you will help exe-cute that plan—that will make it easy for them to re-engage with you. As I mentioned in the chapter on the micromanager, criticiz-ing your boss won't get you very far. Avoid broad generalizations. Instead, provide solutions—such as giving them priority lists and setting up a calendar that only a select few have access to. Offer to reduce your asks. These little steps can go a long way toward get-ting your boss back.

Before you go

▶ Neglect is typically a cyclical process. Long periods of neglect are followed by a buildup of anxiety from feeling out of the loop and, lastly, by attempts to establish top-down control.

▶ There are a lot of reasons why bosses are neglectful, some of which have to do with how they are being managed.

▶ Some bosses aren't getting clear messages from above on what to prioritize, and they have little control over their own time.

▶ Bad management strategies, such as micromanaging, paying attention only to stars, and forgetting what it takes for team members to do their jobs, are additional causes of neglect.

▶ Lots of good bosses fall into a pattern of neglect because they are too generous with time thieves—those pesky people who suck your boss dry looking for advice.

▶ Neglect can happen anytime in a career. Neglectful bosses often overpromise at the interview stage and then underdeliver at the ready-to-launch stage.

▶ Neglectful bosses can be surprisingly knowledgeable about your progress when talking to their bosses. Why? They want to come across as "in the know."

▶ To handle a neglectful boss, your first step is to learn how to need-nudge: make small asks within a reasonable time frame.

▶ Next, try to reduce some of your boss's workload. Prioritize what you need help on and clearly communicate the order of priorities to your boss.

▶ Don't be afraid to ask for help from other experts at work when your boss isn't available. Most bosses will be grateful.

7

The Gaslighter

When Kunal landed a job with Julie, everyone was jealous. Quick-witted and impeccably stylish, Julie was a fearsome thing to behold. At thirty, she was the only woman among the senior leaders in her advertising firm and the youngest by a few decades. Five years ago, she was just another midlevel employee. But raw talent rises quickly, and Julie climbed through the ranks the old-fashioned way. She was nobody's daughter, niece, or lover.

Kunal, on the other hand, was more of a work in progress. His coworkers were thirsty little piranhas, willing to sell a kidney on the black market for a chance to work with Julie. But what Julie craved was a rare combination of traits: she wanted someone who was sharp as a tack, yet naïve when it came to seeing the dark side of human nature. Someone earnest.

Kunal was perfect. From his perspective, there are no jerks at work, just people who have bad days. I would have accused him of toxic positivity.

Julie and Kunal immediately bonded over their shared histories. Like Julie, Kunal didn't grow up in the business world—he worked his way in, inch by inch. They both grew up working class, relying on minimum-wage jobs to pay their way through school. For the first time since he started his career, Kunal felt like he truly belonged.

The story of how Julie gaslit Kunal follows a narrative familiar to those who've been victimized.

Like most victims, Kunal started off enthralled by Julie. Gaslighters don't usually target people who find them weird or gross; they target people who look up to them. There's almost always a power difference, real or imagined, between the gaslighter and their victim. And in the beginning, the victim benefits from that power difference. Julie catapulted Kunal to success. She always gave him credit during team meetings and said wonderful things about him behind his back.

Things were great between them, at first.

Then one day, for whatever reason, Julie's productivity began to slip. Innovative marketing designs became incremental changes. Collective excitement over her ideas waned. We all lose our creative juices sometimes, but to Julie the loss felt permanent. She could feel it closing in on her, like a tumor you know will one day rob you of your breath.

Panicked at the thought of losing it all, she started stealing ideas from people. At first small ones, then big ones. Like the credit stealer, Julie became a foe disguised as a friend. She would offer to help a junior coworker's newest hire, gain access to her coworker's files, then download various markups and documents from that coworker's ideas folder.

"People are surprisingly lax about what they'll share, especially people who look up to you," Julie thought to herself. In the world of advertising, that's a big mistake. Loads of documents, not file protected, were just sitting there waiting for her to steal them.

Julie's method of gaslighting was simple. Steal some material (like an ad markup for eyeshadow), doctor it slightly, and then bring it to Kunal. Kunal would then perfect the ad before Julie presented it to her boss. The process felt truly collaborative—Kunal could feel his creativity blossoming, his fine arts degree finally paying off. He had no idea that Julie didn't do the first step of idea generation on her own.

As they worked through the process, Julie painted a picture of their workplace as one of cutthroat competition. "*Never* show people our work," she told Kunal. "People steal each other's ideas all the time here, and I don't want that to happen to us." When he saw teams of people in the conference room brainstorming, he scoffed. "Those idiots," he thought to himself. "Sharing all their best stuff with each other. I give them a month before they are clawing each other's eyes out over theft accusations." Clearly the earnestness had worn off.

Cut off from the influence of others, Kunal became paranoid, convinced that his work with Julie should remain secret. He stopped socializing with other people—no more coffees or after-work drinks.

People thought his relationship with Julie was strange and insular, but at no point did anyone suspect gaslighting.

In 1938, Patrick Hamilton wrote the play *Gas Light*, about a woman whose husband slowly manipulates her into believing she is going insane. The term "gaslighting" describes a pattern of psychological manipulation whereby one person tries to deceive another into believing in a false reality, often to undermine that person's mental state. Gaslighters differ from everyday liars on one critical dimension: they do it with the intent to deceive on a grand scale.

Perhaps Julie started stealing ideas because she felt trapped. The gaslighting was a means to an end—a way to protect herself from discovery. Or maybe she planned it all along. To me, it doesn't matter. Some gaslighters are sociopaths, others are victims of the situation, but in the end all play the protagonist in their own rich false reality.

In other chapters in this book, I walk through why jerks at work do what they do; knowing the cause of their behavior is important for finding a solution. This chapter is a bit different. Knowing why won't help you get out. In fact, once caught, some gaslighters will try to draw you back in with an excuse for their behavior: "I am so sorry I did this, but I was just so desperate to make progress. You forgive me, right?" The answer should never be yes, no matter how sorry for them they make you feel.

Gaslighting lies outside the realm of typical jerk-at-work behavior; understanding why someone does it should be left to the clinical psychologists. But the good news is, even without a clinical background, you can still see the warning signs and find your way out.

Sneaky behaviors to watch out for

They isolate you by making you feel like part of something special, something only you can know about. Be wary if your boss asks you to join a secret project with a huge payoff or to become a member of a club that only the best and brightest get invited to.

They isolate you by destroying your sense of self-worth. "If it wasn't for me you would have been fired a long time ago" and "No one else thinks you deserved this job, I had to really fight for you" are common things you'll hear from a gaslighter.

They test the waters with their lies—starting off small and working up to the big stuff. Gaslighters love a bit of light, false gossip as a warm-up to the more egregious stuff. "Mark only got here because he used to date the boss's daughter— don't trust anything he says."

They make you question your version of reality, especially your retrospective recall. No, you didn't see your boss access someone else's files or doctor someone else's photos. And you definitely did not witness them walking out of the office with those five boxes marked "confidential." You must be seeing things. Are you feeling okay?

There's this mouse that lives in the desert called the grasshopper mouse that has developed a defense against one of the most painful stings in the animal kingdom—that of the bark scorpion. The mouse uses toxins found in the scorpion's venom to block pain transmission. The more the scorpion strikes, the stronger the block. Then the mouse eats it.

To defeat a gaslighter, you need to become the grasshopper mouse. Gaslighters are cunning, their lies difficult to detect at first. And the hard truth is, the simple act of questioning their honesty can make you weak in the knees. The best defense is to use the gaslighter's tactics against them. In this chapter, I walk you through the steps you need to develop that defense.

But first, you need to find out if you are indeed being gaslit.

ARE YOU BEING LIED TO?

When it comes to lie detection, there's bad news and there's good news. Let's start with the bad news. Scientists have been studying lie detection for decades, and by and large, there is no single set of behaviors reliably associated with lying. Adult liars don't look more anxious or laugh more nervously than truth tellers. Individual liars might have a tell or two, but they vary from person to person. And because there's no standard set of behaviors that give liars away, it's almost impossible to train people to become better lie detectors. Most of us hover around the 54 percent accuracy mark, which is slightly above chance. If you want to become a lie detector at work, you need to throw out the idea that you can tell when someone is lying based on how they look when they're talking to you.

Now for the good news.

Lies that involve complex storytelling do have tells. If someone relates a story that involves elements that don't add up or they switch minor details when they retell it, they might be lying.

Stanford professor David Larcker and University of Chicago professor Anastasia Zakolyukina were interested in how people lie at work, especially when they hold power and the lies have high stakes. They analyzed nearly thirty thousand quarterly earnings conference calls made by CEOs and CFOs. Because they also had data on how well the companies were doing financially, they were able to test which behaviors were associated with dishonest financial reporting.

Here are the three big ones:

1. Liars used the word "we" instead of "I" during the calls to remove personal responsibility.

2. Liars spoke in broad generalizations—using phrases like "they say that" and "everybody knows that"—instead of specific ones ("Tom says that").

3. Liars used overly positive language when things were clearly going downhill.

Positivity is usually a good thing, but not when it's used to overcompensate for losses. Right before Enron imploded, CEO Kenneth Lay told his employees, "I think our core businesses are extremely strong. We have a very strong competitive advantage." Anytime I hear someone use hyperbolic language like this, my bullshit detector goes off.

IF YOU THINK YOU'RE BEING LIED TO, SEEK THE TRUTH

You suspect that you're being lied to. What next? You might be tempted either to extract a confession or gossip about the dishonest person behind their back. These strategies are risky at work. What if you're wrong and they are in fact telling the truth? Falsely accusing someone of lying is a sure way to damage a workplace relationship.

Red flags should be met with further probing, not with accusations that are hard to walk back. If you think you're being lied to, focus on discovering the truth. Seek out hard evidence, such as third-party information and emails that directly contradict the liar. Pay attention to vague statements that are hard to fact-check. I once met a gaslighter who prefaced her reputation-based lies with "everybody says that" (followed by something nasty about whomever she was mad at). Like the liars in David Larcker and Anastasia Zakolyukina's study, her statements were general enough to potentially be true and not specific enough to falsify. I probed for the truth. "Can you tell me exactly who 'everybody' is?" She could not.

When it comes to lying, gaslighters don't dive right into the deep end; they prefer a slow build. Much like a serial killer who observes his victims from afar, gaslighters spend time getting to know you. Whom do you socially connect with and go to for advice? What are your weaknesses? They test the waters by starting off small.

The first time Julie lied to Kunal it was to share her boss's enthusiasm for her new ideas. "I'm getting some great feedback from the top that we are headed in the right direction," she told him. He should have probed to find out who gave her this feedback, but he didn't, so she ramped things up, started stealing more documents. Kunal's naïveté made her feel confident and comfortable. Like a jungle cat stalking its prey, she inched in a little bit closer with each lie he failed to detect.

ARE YOU BEING CUT OFF
FROM OTHER PEOPLE?

For gaslighters, lies and social isolation are like bees and flowers; the first cannot survive without the second. At work, gaslighters typically use one of two social isolation techniques, both of which exploit a basic human need: the need to belong.

The first technique gaslighters use is they make their victims feel special, one of the chosen ones. Like the leaders of terrorist organizations, these gaslighters give their victims a new identity. Victims think they're serving a higher cause, that the work they're doing is more important than whatever everyone else is doing. Outside opinions are unwelcome because they are inferior.

Julie used this strategy on Kunal when he was laboring away on her stolen ideas. They worked together during odd hours to avoid detection, and he was under a strict gag order not to talk about the work. "Clearly our ads are at risk of being stolen," she told him. "We aren't revealing them until they're slapped on a billboard in Times Square."

The second technique that gaslighters use is stripping away their victims' self-worth. Victims are told that no one at work wants them or values them but the gaslighter, and if they complain, they might get fired. They stay isolated out of fear and embarrassment. New employees and those with few social connections are especially vulnerable to this type of gaslighting.

I've witnessed this heartbreaking form of gaslighting firsthand. Katina was energetic and full of ideas when she was hired, but six months in, she turned aloof and distant. "How are you doing here? How's your relationships with Taylor?" I asked (Taylor was her sharp-tongued boss). She robotically told me that things were great, she was learning a lot.

It didn't feel right, so I started digging. Taylor had a revolving door of talent; most of her young employees left within a year of being hired. But no complaints were filed, so she stayed off the radar. Over time, I learned that Taylor isolated her victims by slowly eating away at their self-esteem, nibble by nibble. Like the lies, her insults started off small. She told Katina that she needed to work on her accent if she wanted to be taken seriously. Embarrassed, Katina stopped speaking up in meetings. The lies escalated from there, most of which served to further isolate Katina. Taylor would say things such as "No one wants to read your work until I approve it; your writing is atrocious" and "People think you're strange and socially inappropriate; you shouldn't go to the company party this Friday." Reporting the abuse was out of the question—Taylor told her that if she did, her reputation as an ungrateful whiner would follow her to her next position. Like those before her, Katina ended up quitting not long after she started.

ARE YOU BEING ASKED TO DO UNETHICAL THINGS?

Watch out for bosses who get you to do naughty little deeds for them, starting with the smallest of asks. Gaslighters are well aware of the slippery-slope phenomenon when it comes to unethical behavior at work: it's much easier to persuade people to commit small immoral acts, which increase incrementally, than it is to persuade them to commit big ones.

It's a lot like what Stanley Milgram and his team did to the participants in his famous shock studies from the early 1960s. They were instructed to shock another participant every time he got an answer wrong on some bogus test. No one was actually shocked in the study—the man people believed they were shocking worked for Milgram—but a large percentage of the participants were willing to go up to the maximum voltage. Why? Because they were asked to increase the shocks little by little, not all at once.

Don't be a participant in a Stanley Milgram experiment.

Your gaslighter will start off small—"Can you grab that folder off your coworker's desk they left behind?" "Can you clean up those data for me?" But in time, they'll work you up to the big stuff.

I've been called "uptight" and "a real stickler for the rules" by would-be gaslighters. To me, these were red flags. Your boss should not talk like a high school bully.

WHEN GASLIGHTING IS MOST LIKELY TO OCCUR

People often ask me what social situations they should avoid if they don't want to be gaslit. The answer to the question is more of a when than a where.

WHEN YOU'RE UP CLOSE AND PERSONAL

Gaslighting is intimate business, best done at a safe distance from prying eyes and ears. The cleverest gaslighter I knew, Gary, was careful not to document any of his dirty deeds. When he set up a meeting, he wouldn't even say what it was about. Lies were delivered only face-to-face. Gary met his demise when his employee

Jasna, suspecting she was being lied to, started taking meticulous notes during their private meetings. She then sent the notes to Gary afterward. "Thanks for the meeting today. Just wanted to send you my notes on what we discussed." Sensing his vulnerability, Gary moved on. Record keeping is kryptonite to gaslighters.

WHEN BELIEVING THEIR LIES MEANS A BETTER FUTURE FOR YOU

Michael was a scientist and part of something special. For the past several months, he and his boss, Scarlet, had been conducting secret experiments—work too important to tell anyone about—and now they sat huddled together at her computer, poring through the data. "Once this work is published, you will have job offers left and right," she told him. The academic job market sucks, so this was music to Michael's ears.

Scarlet stepped away for a moment to make a call, and Michael ran a few quick analyses on the data. To his surprise, the data were a garbled mess. Registering his puzzled look, Scarlet quicky scooted him out of his seat. "Oh, this must be the wrong file. Why don't you take a break and come back in an hour? I'll have everything sorted out." When he returned, the data were magically cooperative.

Gaslighters take advantage of every vulnerability at their disposal. Beware of the boss who tries to sell you on a reality that feels too good to be true. Most of us think that gaslighting feels like abuse, but that need not be the case. Sometimes it feels like a mirage in the desert.

WHEN YOU'RE NOT AROUND TO DEFEND YOURSELF

Smart gaslighters think two steps ahead, planning for the possibility that one day, their victims will break free and try to burn the house down. To prepare, they will build a case against you. And when the time comes, they strike.

There are lots of tragic stories I could tell to illustrate this point. But my favorite involved Lucy, the master of vindication. Lucy was four years into her gaslighting adventure with her boss, Aaron, when one serendipitous evening, while out to dinner with her wife and friends, she learned that one of the friends used to work for Aaron.

It was the most eye-opening meal of her life.

Exhausted from the abuse and full of rage, Lucy put in her two-week notice, then went door-to-door trash-talking Aaron to all who would listen. (I don't recommend this strategy in general, but sometimes a little comeuppance is in order.) Smelling blood in the water (his own), Aaron called a meeting of company leaders. Prepared for this day, he delivered a speech describing how unprofessional and abusive Lucy was during their four-year relationship.

It probably would have worked if it wasn't the third time he tried it. Aaron was a serial gaslighter.

Lucy's case is an extreme one, but rest assured, your gaslighter will collect dirt on you in case the day comes when he needs to hit the eject button.

HOW CAN I ESCAPE
A RELATIONSHIP WITH
A GASLIGHTER?

Escaping the grasp of a gaslighter is like freeing yourself from a spider's web—after you've been bound, paralyzed, and readied for consumption, that is. It's a tough job, but not impossible! To pull it off, you will need a lot of patience and a willingness to go outside your comfort zone. You also need time. Again, patience is key here.

RECLAIM YOUR RECALL OF EVENTS

Deep down, Kunal knew things weren't adding up with Julie. The pace at which she created new content was unbelievable. Her panic over him using a company printer seemed excessive. And on one particularly late night, he could swear he saw her logged in to a co-worker's account. The next day she told him he imagined it. He wasn't so sure.

To keep their grip on you, gaslighters create an alternative version of reality, and they'll do pretty much anything to preserve it.

There will be times when you question their behavior or find holes in their logic, but they might be fleeting. Do not wait until after the event is over to question your sanity. Our memories are flawed and messy even without a gaslighter interfering with them. Add the gaslighter to the mix, and by the next day, you'll have no idea what actually happened.

The moment you think something doesn't feel right, write it down. Take pictures of it. Record yourself talking about it. Do whatever you can to preserve it. These small records will become invaluable when you're ready to open up to other people. They might even give you the confidence to do so. "See, I have evidence," always makes me feel more comfortable confronting a problem.

BUILD UP YOUR SOCIAL NETWORK, LITTLE BY LITTLE

The most important step you need to take when confronting a gaslighter is the very thing your gaslighter spent months conditioning you to be afraid of: turning to other people for help. At this point, you might feel like you have very little social network left. The thought of reaching out to people makes your heart pound and your palms sweat.

On top of these emotions, trauma can affect the basic ways we process social information. One thing that survivors of war, car accidents, and intimate partner violence all have in common is that they show a *threat bias* when it comes to reading other people's emotions. They think, for example, that neutral faces are angry, and when they encounter welcoming faces, they don't process them as quickly and efficiently as they process angry ones. There might be a world of people at work ready to help you, but after living under a gaslighter's grip, when you look around, all you see is scorn and contempt.

Knowing that you have this bias is the first step to overcoming it. There's a good chance that no one at work knows you're being gaslit. Remember, gaslighting is intimate business, and if you aren't talking about it, neither is your gaslighter.

To overcome this bias, I suggest building up your network slowly, starting with the people who are closest to you—past friends or allies from the beforetime. Pretend you're the new kid in school determined to become prom queen by year's end. What is the best strategy to gain popularity? Start locally by gaining the trust of people who are close to you in status or position—those whom you have the most contact with. Then slowly build your network, little by little.

Some victims are tempted to shoot straight to the top once they realize they've been gaslit—to find the most powerful person they can, report their experience, and then hope for change. I've rarely seen this strategy work, and here's why. You were tormented in private. While you were stuck in a cage somewhere, your gaslighter was out networking with powerful people. Hell, they might even be one of those powerful people. Don't assume that people will immediately be on your aside. You will need your social network to do some of the convincing for you.

FIND A SOCIAL REFERENT

Princeton University psychologist Betsy Paluck studies how to reduce bullying behavior in high schools. She's found that the best way to change norms around bullying is to find a few key people who are well-connected, called *social referents,* and directly target them with anti-bullying campaigns. Social referents might be popular, likable, or have a lot of status—there are many reasons why someone is a social referent. The key feature is that they get a lot of attention from their peers.

Five characteristics of social referents

They know a lot of people at work—from the tech team who set up your computer to the long-standing leaders in the organization.

They know the norms of the workplace—including what's acceptable behavior and what's not.

They've observed a lot of action at work. They were around when your boss had that falling-out with his old boss and also five years later, when the two became best friends again.

Other people have a good sense of how they respond to things. Everybody knows what your social referent does when someone gets interrupted at work (they cut in) or gets locked out of their office (they know a guy with a skeleton key).

They are the only shared connection between lots of different people. No one else at work goes out to dinner with the head of sales one night and the manager of the on-site coffee shop the next, except a social referent.

Once you've started to build back your social network, try to find a social referent; someone who not only is on your side but is good at bringing people in power together to talk about your problem.

Remember my friend Michael the scientist, whose boss Scarlet persuaded him to run secret experiments with her? This is what he did. Michael found another scientist at work, Vince, who wasn't part of his team and didn't do research in the same area. Vince had a reputation for being reasonable and levelheaded and, most important, people listened to him. He didn't have the power to fire Michael's boss, Scarlet, but he was good at sounding the alarm bells; if he said there was a problem, the ears of the power players perked up. Once Vince got the ball rolling, Michael moved to a new team, and protections were put in place to shield him from retaliation.

APPROACH PEOPLE WITH THE INTENT OF ASKING FOR FEEDBACK

I took a leadership training course at New York University, and one of the most useful things I learned is how to address problems indirectly when the direct route ruffles too many feathers. Sometimes this means finding the right framing to appeal to people.

Walking into someone's office and leading with, "Thanks for seeing me; I would like to talk about the torture I've endured at the hands of your coworker Bob for the last three months" might not get you to where you want to be—at least not initially. Instead, approach people with a smaller problem you have—for instance, the lack of feedback your gaslighter has given you over those last three months.

When Kunal first realized that things weren't adding up with Julie, he reached out to a few contacts from the past. "I know we haven't talked in a while, but I'm hoping to get some feedback," he would say. He talked a little about the types of interactions he was having at work (mostly one-on-one with Julie, not very often with other team members), and he asked what other senior leaders thought of his relationship with Julie. The responses he got ranged from "No one knows much about you, but we trust what Julie says" to "Kunal, something isn't right here—are you comfortable with me bringing this issue up to other leaders?"

To Kunal, this strategy felt safe. If word got back to Julie that he was asking around for feedback, she had little to retaliate against. It also helped him find a social referent—the person who brought the leaders together to talk about his problem.

WAIT TO CONFRONT YOUR GASLIGHTER HEAD-ON

Confronting problems at work is important. In fact, most of the chapters in this book focus on how to confront a jerk at work in a healthy and productive way. But gaslighters fall into a different category. Telling yours that you know they're lying won't make them stop. They might double down on their behavior, change their lying strategy, or lash out at you in an unpredictable way. Remember, while you were being gaslit, your gaslighter was out in the world creating a reality that you know very little about. They probably also put some steps in place—such as Scarlet saving files of fake data that Michael created—to make people at least question your role.

When Julie's lies were discovered, the first thing she did was turn on Kunal. He had been editing stolen material for several months at this point, and from her perspective, he was just as guilty as she was. "You can't just walk away from this! You worked on those stolen ads too!" she said.

Julie had no proof that Kunal was the one who sold her out, but she suspected as much. The more he debated the veracity of her statements, the more she doubled down. Eventually, he realized it was best to stay quiet and document her lies until his exit strategy was in place. Kunal's best weapon was silence; the less insight Julie had into what was going on behind the scenes, the better. And the more she lied, the more documentation he had. The key was switching his mind-set from one of blind to acceptance to constant suspicion. I rarely recommend the strategy of all-out avoidance, but the most effective way to escape a gaslighter without getting hurt is to back out of the relationship slowly, not throw a grenade at it.

WHAT SHOULD YOU DO IF YOU'RE APPROACHED BY A GASLIGHTER?

Nothing can kill workplace morale quite like an unpunished gaslighter. Gaslighting is a psychologically damaging process to go through and, like divorce, people pick sides. Once the full scope of Julie's behavior was revealed, senior leadership had to act swiftly to contain the reputational damage to the company, while Julie went door-to-door and told people all the ways Kunal was really the mastermind.

If this happens to you, try not to be a vehicle for the possible gaslighter's gossip. If you aren't sure whose side you're on, just stay quiet. Let their gossip die with you.

Remember, social ostracism can come in many forms, including a failure to commiserate. One of the most effective strategies that Kunal's social referent implemented was to get everyone on the same page with how to respond when Julie approached them. Everyone agreed not to indulge her attempts to smear Kunal and to minimize unnecessary contact with her. Conversation with Julie felt stilted and awkward, but she quickly learned that her time was best served venting to people other than her work colleagues.

If possible, remove as many levers of power from the gaslighter as you can. Try to prevent this person from becoming a rule maker or system overseer. Don't allow gaslighters to have access to information about other employees whom they could potentially gaslight.

I SUSPECT MY COWORKER IS BEING GASLIT. WHAT SHOULD I DO?

When I talk to people about what gaslighting looks like at work, one of the more common responses is, "Oh SHIT. I think my coworker is being gaslit." This can be a tough realization to have. What are you supposed do when you suspect, but don't know, that someone is being abused by a gaslighter at work?

As I mentioned earlier, the red flags of gaslighting are often more about the lack of information you can get out of victims than the presence of it. Remember Katina—the woman whose boss, Taylor, gaslit her by constantly insulting her work and making her feel too insecure to speak up? The red flag with Katina was her sudden withdrawal—and, quite frankly, her lack of willingness to say *anything* substantial about her boss.

If you have a coworker who won't join in on the usual collaborative projects, seems uninterested or unwilling to connect with people inside or outside of work, and hangs out *only* with the boss, then you might want to do a little bit of digging. I would start by doing the very things I've instructed victims of gaslighters to do in this chapter:

▶ Offer to be a social referent or connect this person with someone who is.

▶ Help buffer this person from the gaslighter by offering to create physical distance and social distance, maybe by moving workstations or inviting them to group lunches with other coworkers.

▶ If the potential victim is willing to talk about it but not necessarily to you, then connect them with someone who, in an official capacity, is required to keep their conversation confidential. Victims of gaslighters often worry that they will get caught gossiping about or bad-mouthing their boss—and they've spent months being conditioned not to trust anyone—so offering to provide help with taking the formal route to reporting the abuse can help quell this concern.

And as tempting as it might be, try not to let word get out that this person is being gaslit. The gossip will likely get back to the gaslighter, who will then go into full self-protection mode. The longer you can stave off that stage of the process, the better.

CONFRONTING THE CASUAL LIAR

Clearly not all liars are gaslighters, but lots of us have had experience with people who have some of the flavors of a gaslighter—the dishonesty, the tendency to control—but aren't the whole package. Maybe you have a boss who isn't interested in baking up a full-blown alternative reality, but they do small things, such as discredit someone they're jealous of through a series of small lies. Bulldozers do this a lot, and so do kiss up/kick downers.

Should you confront these people? I would first start by asking yourself, What is the nature of the lies? If they are personal ("Did you hear that Steve asked out Jane and she laughed at him?"), let it die with you. Don't respond. I'm sure Steve would appreciate that little piece of gossip dying out.

The tellers of these lies aren't always motivated by a desire to damage people's reputations. I once knew a liar who spread all sorts of small lies about people, mostly with the intent of building camaraderie with the person she was lying to. The content of the lie wasn't important; she just wanted to share and laugh with someone.

If the lie is work related, then seek the truth. Follow the steps I've outlined above.

If you're bold, you can confront these liars one-on-one, but I think a more fruitful strategy (and one that's more damaging to the liar) is to find a social referent or a group of coworkers who are also on the receiving end of these lies. Once you've done some truth seeking, you can confront the liar as a group. There's power in numbers, and your goal is to communicate that this behavior "isn't what we do here."

Lying can become normative fast, and you want to stop that from happening. In the case of my gossipy coworker, we added another layer of punishment. We socially ostracized her until she stopped lying. No invites to dinners or after-work happy hours. Basically, a grown-up version of time-out.

Gaslighters are the most psychologically damaging—and the most complicated—jerk at work. They have a wealth of skills at their disposal, including some we hate to admit they have, such as charisma and the ability to make us feel special, which makes defeating them a challenge. The biggest barrier that victims face in overcoming a gaslighter is themselves; it is hard to admit that you've sunk months, sometimes years, of your life into playing a supporting role in your gaslighter's false reality. Allies at work, including friends, social referents, and other leaders, are absolutely critical in extracting people from a gaslighter's grip. Forming a layer of protection is key, as is cutting off the gaslighter from access to their victims. Once you get over the hump of believing that no one cares about you at work and no one values you, you too can get your life back and thrive after surviving a gaslighter.

Before You Go

▶ Lying at work is common. We tell altruistic lies to make social interactions go smoothly and self-protecting lies to bolster our image and cover up our small indiscretions.

▶ There are no good ways of detecting lies from watching how people behave. At best you will be slightly above chance at guessing whether someone is lying or telling the truth simply by how they behave when they talk to you. The best way to become a good lie detector at work is to seek out the truth.

▶ Complex lies do have giveaways. If someone avoids personal responsibility (using "we" or "they" when "I" is more appropriate), describes things using vague language instead of specifics, and appears overly positive, then it's time to seek the truth.

▶ Gaslighters differ from everyday liars in that they try to isolate their victims. They typically take one of two approaches: one, they make their victims feel like part of something special; or two, they make their victims question their self-worth.

▶ Gaslighting occurs in private, often out of earshot. Savvy gaslighters are careful not to document their lies. Don't expect yours to leave a paper trail.

▶ Not all gaslighting feels like abuse—some gaslighters take advantage of victims by selling them on a reality that feels too good to be true.

▶ Gaslighters are careful to cover their tracks. When they aren't gaslighting you, they are busy trying to impress powerful people to protect themselves from future reputational damage.

▶ Removing yourself from a gaslighter's grip requires the help of other people. Slowly build up your social network, starting with those closest to you in status and rank, and find a social referent—someone who gets a lot of attention from their peers and is broadly connected to many people.

▶ If opening up about your experience feels daunting, start small by asking for some general feedback.

▶ Once a gaslighter is discovered, it is important for those in power not to become enablers. If a gaslighter approaches you to gossip, don't indulge them. Gaslighters will often try to sabotage their victims through gossip.

Conclusion

On February 18, 2021, the *Perseverance* rover landed on Mars, starting its mission to look for ancient microbial life on the red planet. Rob Donnelly, a flight electronics engineer at NASA's Jet Propulsion Laboratory, helped put it there.

"I spent three and a half years of my life on something that would operate for ten seconds," Rob told me. As the FPGA verification lead for the Lander Vision System, Rob's job was to make sure that when *Perseverance* reached Mars, it could figure out where it was in order to avoid landing hazards. On Earth, we use GPS to figure out location, but on Mars there is no GPS, so *Perseverance* uses computer vision. Rob's team spent a lot of time in the simulation stage before they got to the hardware stage, working out all possible worst-case scenarios. On Mars, the terrain is rough. One wrong move and *Perseverance* could easily have landed on a giant rock, shattering itself to bits.

Those ten seconds were arguably the most exhilarating of Rob's career. I watched the live landing, which showed both the rover on Mars and the faces of the engineers and scientists who built it. In my twenty-or-so years as a social psychologist, I've never seen emotion contagion like this. The anxiety and uncertainty—and then the elation—were as thick as fog. So too was the sense of camaraderie.

When the landing was declared a success, there wasn't a dry eye in the room. For Rob, the high felt endless: "My body was on Earth, but my head was on Mars. I couldn't get any work done. It took me a solid week to come down."

Understandable for a man who helped launch one of the most important scientific breakthroughs of a generation.

For those life-changing ten seconds, Rob worked with the same people, day in and day out, for three and a half years. There were setbacks, and conflicts, and all the other things that make working in teams tough. The people who put *Perseverance* on Mars might be some of the best scientists and engineers in the world, but they are still human. And humans argue over things such as who should get credit for a team's success and who's been free riding.

For most of us, sustained conflict at work causes stress and anxiety and interferes with our ability to get stuff done. But for the *Perseverance* team, sustained conflict just wasn't an option. Neither was leaving when things got tough. There was so much expertise involved and the timeline was so tight, if someone behaved like a jerk at work, the problem had to be fixed immediately.

Imagine if Rob started kissing up and kicking down two years into the job. Could his boss fire him for being rude to the other electronics engineers and bring someone new in with eighteen months left before launch? Probably not. The spacecraft alone cost more than $2 billion. Replacing the person responsible for making sure it could see, simply because he snapped at too many people, wasn't a viable option. (Not that it needed to be; Rob is lovely. But you get my point.)

One might think that with such a high-stakes project, it would behoove NASA and the Jet Propulsion Laboratory to bring in the big guns and hire some high-paid social psychologists to massage away conflict the minute it cropped up. But they didn't need to. Rob and his team used the same strategies I recommend in this book to prevent and manage conflict. And none of them cost a million dollars, or hours and hours of precious time, to implement.

"There was a lot of hierarchy on teams, lots of structure. No one person knows all the fine details of the spacecraft," Rob said. He told me that ideas were often "in the air," as it is with a lot of creative, fast-moving teams. And like most hierarchical teams, determining credit was often tough.

"There were times when people didn't do a great job of credit granting," recounted Rob, "occasions where I felt individual contributions could have been better represented."

One thing Rob noticed was the overuse of the word "we" to refer to a team's work during meetings with the boss, when it felt more appropriate to grant credit to individual team members. And sometimes, he said, "people were excluded altogether with phrasing like, 'The problem was X and the solution was Y.'"

Rob's team quickly solved this issue with just a few small practices that made people feel included and appreciated. They would echo the contributions of their team members and make it clear to the boss who did what. They kept track of individual contributions, no matter how chaotic things got. This way, no one could free-ride and no one could overclaim credit. Everyone was fairly recognized for their contributions.

"There were one or two people who were the spokespersons for teamwork," explained Rob. "When they reported status [jobs that were done that week], they would work in the names of all the individuals who contributed. Instead of saying, 'We identified the problem, developed the fix, and verified the fix,' the spokesperson would say, 'Person A identified the problem. Person B developed the fix, and Person C verified the fix.' Good spokespeople would then tell a short story that captured the challenges the team encountered, highlighting the individuals who contributed to overcoming those challenges."

Rob's team learned that the simple act of moving from "we" to "Person A" was enough to get people to feel like they were getting the credit they deserved. Small moves such as these, done early and often, prevented big problems from festering down the line. And the best part was, they were painless and costless to implement. Anyone could adopt them.

Rob's work could be stressful and the stakes were high, so whenever mistakes were made, it was easy to point fingers.

"There was a point in the project where we knew we weren't going to finish everything in time," he said."We could have kept on the same course, making the mountain smaller, but when we got to the end of the runway, we would have still had a mountain of unfinished work."

Lots of teams would struggle at this stage. A bulldozer could easily come in and take over, demand that things went their way. Free riders could get away with doing nothing. But Rob's team had put so much effort into identifying these problems early on that they were able to solve them quickly and efficiently. They prioritized what was essential, then delegated the work. And when the work was done, they went back to their relationships: "We met once a month for happy hour. We celebrated Diwali together. When things got tough at work, we were all fighting the issues instead of each other."

Some people might think that the scientists and engineers who put the *Perseverance* rover on Mars must have focused entirely on work for three and a half years. There was no way they had time to focus on their relationships with one another.

Wrong.

These folks knew, like you and me, that jerk-at-work problems can be the death of a team. And luckily for you and me, it doesn't take a rocket scientist to solve them. It's about looking out for warning signs, understanding why someone behaves the way they do, and learning how to open the lines of communication so you can solve the problem quickly and with as little stress as possible.

That way you have time for the real rocket science.

ACKNOWLEDGMENTS

There are several people I want to thank who gave me the inspiration I needed to write this book. To Jay Van Bavel, who was convinced (before I was) that I had a book in me, and to Heidi Grant, who encouraged me to write about a topic that is stressful and scary to people, using humor. Without these two, I never would have had the confidence to write this book.

I will be forever indebted to my son, Matty, who kept me inspired during lockdown with his own jerk-at-work tales of life in the second grade. I learned of the "credit stealer" who stole his Lego House idea and the "bulldozer" who insisted on reading to the class at every story time.

Many people inspired the stories in this book. I thank my mom, who entertained me with her own tales of workplace woe; my brother, who convinced me that the "computer guy" (him) is the most socially connected person at work; and Janet Ahn, whose stories about and advice on how to handle jerk-at-work problems were invaluable.

I thank Rob Donnelly, who graciously shared his experience working on *Perseverance*, and Khalil Smith, who gave me advice on how to improve my jerk-at-work questionnaires.

I owe a debt of gratitude to my students (past and present) and my research collaborators. None of the research I talk about in this book would have been possible without them. To Kate Thorson and Oana Dumitru, whose insights into how to study the dynamics between people—while measuring their behaviors and recording their physiology—brought our research to life. To Chadly Stern, who thought creatively about how to use chairs to measure interpersonal distance, and to Joe Magee, Lindy Gullett, and Sarah Gordon, who figured out how to manipulate similarity between people in complex social situations. I thank Gavin Kilduff and Siyu Yu, who graciously invited me to be part of their research on status.

To Wendy Mendes, who taught me everything I know about creating experiments that feel like real life. To my teachers, Dave Kenny and Jack Dovidio, who gave me the kind of mentoring that I can only aspire to give my students.

I want to thank my agent, Nat Jacks, who gave me detailed, thoughtful feedback along the way that shaped this book, and always made me feel confident in my ideas. To my editors, Leah Trouwborst and Nina Rodríguez-Marty, who gave this book an attention to detail that I know is hard to find. Without the three of you, this book never would have come to life.

What Type of Jerk Do I Have at Work?

Is your jerk a coworker or a boss? For coworker, proceed. For a boss, go to the next flowchart.

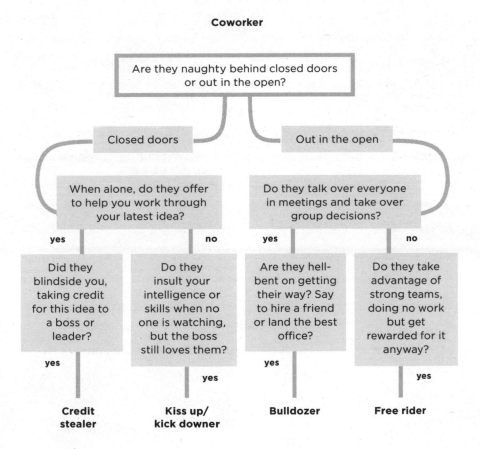

Coworker

Are they naughty behind closed doors or out in the open?

Closed doors

Out in the open

When alone, do they offer to help you work through your latest idea?

Do they talk over everyone in meetings and take over group decisions?

yes — no

yes — no

Did they blindside you, taking credit for this idea to a boss or leader?

Do they insult your intelligence or skills when no one is watching, but the boss still loves them?

Are they hell-bent on getting their way? Say to hire a friend or land the best office?

Do they take advantage of strong teams, doing no work but get rewarded for it anyway?

yes

yes

yes

yes

Credit stealer

Kiss up/ kick downer

Bulldozer

Free rider

What Type of Jerk Do I Have at Work?

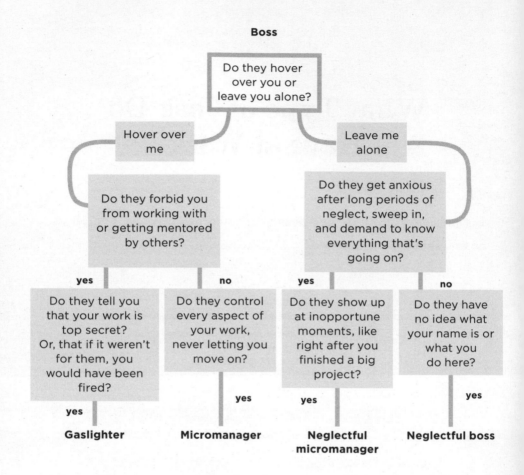

Quiz 1

Am I a Jerk at Work?

Welcome to the "Am I a Jerk at Work?" quiz! Each question is designed to assess how you would respond to a series of tricky, hypothetical workplace situations. I recommend you take it twice: once before you read the book and again after. You might see some interesting changes in how you respond. At the end, you'll find out whether you're a conniving trickster, classic jerk, just going through the motions—or have been an ideal coworker all along.

At the end of the quiz, there are two parts. In part 1, I provide a scoring sheet and describe each of the four types. In part 2, I provide an answer guide where I walk through my logic and explain what each answer says about your behavior at work. The goal of this quiz isn't to make you feel pigeonholed into one category. In fact, most of you will have answers that fall into all four categories.

The goal is to open you up to new perspectives on how to handle jerk-at-work problems.

Often it is easier to talk about jerk-at-work problems with your team members, direct reports, and bosses when they are hypothetical, so the quiz is meant to stimulate discussion. You can answer for yourself as an assessment tool or have people answer it from the perspective of others at work.

The answers people provide can also reveal a lot about a company's culture. If everyone in your organization is leaning toward conniving trickster in their answers, well, that tells you something about the competitive vibe among people.

Have fun and bring your answers to the next company party. It might spark some interesting conversation!

Question 1

You recently started a new job selling shirts. You're an expert folder—every shirt on the table looks perfect—which is why your boss hired you. One day, you notice that your new team member, Gavin, is making a mistake. His shirts are sloppy; clearly no one trained him how to fold. Your boss is within earshot, overseeing your work together. What do you do?

    a.   Correct Gavin loudly so the boss can hear you. It's important she knows *you* know what you're doing.

    b.   Correct Gavin privately when the two of you are alone later, making sure he doesn't feel stupid in the process.

    c.   Do nothing—Gavin's mistake is not your problem.

    d.   Don't say anything to Gavin but approach your boss at a later time to express your concerns about him. If he can't fold shirts, what else is he bad at?

Question 2

This week, everyone at work gets their year-end bonus. At your job in sales, the bonus is a direct reflection of how much you sold that year. To celebrate, everyone goes to the big company party on the day bonuses are handed out. What's your party plan?

    a.   Approach everyone at the party and ask what their bonuses are. There's only one reason why you're here, and it's to figure out who the winners and losers are.

    b.   There's only one person whose bonus you care about: Rena. Rena is your competition for the VP of sales job, and you need to know how close she is to catching up to you. You ask her directly what she got this year.

    c.   Money is a private thing. Don't ask, don't tell.

    d.   Make a beeline for the boss and ask her where you stand relative to everyone else; it's important to get this info right from the source. And if she evades you, ask again.

Question 3

You're an architect, and you've joined a new team that will be designing a mansion for an eccentric millionaire. It's the first day, and everyone is getting settled for the first in-person meeting. The boss is out of town this week and has told your group to get started in his absence. What's your move?

    a.   Give a speech about how experienced you are and offer to lead the team. You know exactly what it will take to bring this mansion to life, and that won't happen unless you're in charge.

    b.   Suggest that everyone goes around and says their name and years of experience. It's good to know who the competition will be for "best in show."

    c.   Say nothing the whole time. It's best to let others figure out the plan moving forward.

    d.   Work with a handful of others to get the group focused on a set of goals for the day; you hate meetings that are inefficient and this one will drag on forever if you let it.

Question 4

You're up for a big promotion and the other person being considered is Kevin. Kevin treats you with respect and you typically get along, but lately you've been feeling pretty competitive with him. You know that your boss loves Kevin, and this makes you nervous. You:

    a.   Approach your boss and make sure she's aware of Kevin's shortcomings. You want her to have the full picture so she can make the most informed decision.

    b.   Approach one of the other leaders who will be deciding on who gets the promotion. You zero in on a well-connected power player named Siena with a talent for swaying opinions and tell her about Kevin's shortcomings.

    c.   Put your time and effort into showcasing your skills, especially during moments when Kevin isn't around to showcase his.

    d.   Just be yourself and let the bosses decide. No need to try to flex this late in the game.

Question 5

You and your coworker Kiera are on a team together, and your project requires a lot of creativity. The team meetings are intense—lots of ideas are thrown around, and at the end, the team lists the top five ideas to bring to the boss. At one point, Kiera has an insight that feels remarkably similar to the one you had five minutes ago. No one credits you for the idea, but "Kiera's" idea lands on the top five list. You:

a. Chastise the group. It is not that hard to tell the difference between you and Kiera. You don't even look alike.

b. Say nothing but stew in anger.

c. Share your experience of feeling shortchanged with the group but also offer some solutions, such as coming up with a few ways to keep track of who said what.

d. Approach Kiera and ask her why she didn't correct the group when they gave her credit for your idea. That was her job to do, and she failed.

Question 6

You're at a party thrown by your boss to celebrate your big promotion. For the last six months, you and your mentee, Max, have been working together to close a big deal. Max claims that you got here only because you stole all his ideas and never gave him credit for them. You can see him seething by the bar. What do you do?

a. Ignore Max and have fun. Why does he have to be such a party pooper? He'd better get over this by Monday.

b. Give a big speech thanking Max for a whole bunch of things he didn't do to create the appearance of support. If he complains about you again, he'll come across as ungrateful.

c. Bite the bullet and have the awkward conversation with Max where you sort out who did what. It's better to clear the air than to let things simmer.

   d.   Find all the socially connected people and make sure they
        know that Max is full of shit. How dare he try to smear
        your reputation?

Question 7

Your boss promised you that when you relocated offices, you would
get a nice big one with natural light and vaulted ceilings. But on the
day of the big move, you learn that your office is small and awkward, and the office you were promised was given to a newcomer
named Alexander. Your boss tells you to sort out the issue with
Alexander yourself. What do you do?

   a.   Tell Alexander that this was a mistake. His office is the
        awkward one, yours is the nice one. Then ask for the keys.
   b.   Subtly express to your boss that if he doesn't sort out of
        the office issue, you might lose interest in helping him
        with that new initiative he's excited about.
   c.   Complain about your boss to the CEO, John. The two of you
        have kids on the same softball team and you're buddies
        now. Surely John can fix this.
   d.   Approach Alexander and feel him out for a deal. In ex-
        change for the nice office, offer to connect him with a few
        folks who can help him learn some tricks of the trade, such
        as how to make sure his voice is heard in meetings and
        which days of the week are the best to schedule a talk with
        the boss.

Question 8

Your boss asked you to join a group on planning the transition
back to in-person work. You care about this issue a lot. The first
job of the group is to collect data to see what people's opinions are.

You're the only person with the expertise to collect the data and process it. Your boss turns to you with a look of desperation. What do you do?

a. Offer to create a workplace survey and share the data with everyone. Keep the passwords to yourself, along with the instructions on how to process the data. Your survey, your business.

b. Offer to help train two other people to collect the data and process it. You don't want to be the only person who knows how to do this stuff.

c. Ignore your boss's requests. It's his problem that he didn't hire anyone else who knows what they're doing.

d. Offer to create the survey, but only if you get to run the meetings and make up all the procedures. This survey will be a lot of work, so you should be offered some power in return.

Question 9

You've been feeling really burned out at work lately—your team is full of free riders who do nothing. Just when you were ready to quit, your boss comes to you with good news: you've been put on a new team full of conscientious team players who know one another well. What's your first step?

a. Coast and let everyone else do the hard work. You deserve a break.

b. You've been burned before, and it won't happen again. Ask your boss to rank everyone from best to worst employee at the end of the month, and then send out the list to the group. Suggest that those at the bottom lose their bonus unless they can move up the list in the next month.

c. Ask the new team if you can work together to come up with a list of tasks for everyone to complete. At the end of the month, compare what people agreed to do with what they actually did.

d. Agree to do the tough jobs that require your expertise but secretly off-load the easy ones to your new intern. You've struggled to find jobs for her, and no one needs to know. She'll be gone in two months anyway.

Question 10

About five months ago, you hired Irene to help run your cupcake company. Every time you stop by the bakery, Irene is out in front, greeting customers and making sure every cupcake is frosted to perfection. However, a few of the bakers have complained to you that Irene acts like this only when you're around. When you're gone, she sits in the back licking frosting off spoons. What do you do?

a. Tell your bakers to stop complaining. Not all problems are best solved by gossiping to the boss.

b. Fire Irene immediately. You're not paying her to eat the goods. Then put a big sign up that reads, "If you eat on the job, that cupcake will be your last." It's important to make it clear that this type of behavior won't be tolerated.

c. Have the team (including Irene) come up with a checklist of what their tasks are for the day. Include the items "Did you do any extra work you didn't plan for" and "Did you notice anyone else doing extra work?" In a week, go through the answers. Your goal is to see if people are systematically picking up Irene's slack.

d. Tell the team that to discourage free riders, everyone is going to have a quota of fifty cupcakes a day—baked and sold.

And that includes Irene. You'll come back in a month and evaluate how everyone is doing.

Question 11

You've recently been promoted to a manager position, and your job is to oversee the work of ten people. The most senior among them, Jesse, has been given the job you had last week. You were excellent at your old job, and you hope Jesse will succeed. What's the first thing you do in your new role?

a.   Spend your time carefully overseeing everything Jesse does. You want to make sure he's as good at the job as you were.

b.   Create a new role—a leader that Jesse reports to—who will fill you in on how Jesse is doing. The more people who can oversee Jesse the better.

c.   Have a conversation with Jesse about his long-term goals and your short-term needs. What is he hoping to get out of this job, and what do you need him to accomplish? Then set up a weekly timeline.

d.   Turn your attention toward impressing *your* boss. You would be happy to see Jesse thrive, but you're confident he has the skills to do so on his own.

Question 12

You work at a resort hotel and it's busy season—at least a hundred summer workers are on the clock, waiting to serve poolside drinks and teach tourists how to surf. But today there was a huge rainstorm. Everyone is sitting around with nothing to do. As a manager you:

a.   Find something—anything—for these people to do. Even if that means triple washing the furniture by the pool.

b. Gather everyone up for a little training session on how to improve their customer service skills. Why not spend this time learning something useful?

c. Open the pool bar, set up a poker tournament, and get yourself a massage at the hotel spa.

d. Spend your time chatting with the workers to find out the hotel gossip—whom do they like and whom do they hate? Share a few fun details yourself to get them to open up to you.

Question 13

Your employee Ester complains to you that you're smothering her. "You send me four emails an hour. If you want me to get work done, I can't be spending all my time responding to you." How do you respond to Ester?

a. If Ester was better at her job, you wouldn't have to remind her to do things four times an hour. You tell her this.

b. Immediately replace Ester with someone who treats you with respect. On day one, lecture this person on what happens when you write snarky emails to the boss.

c. Sit down with Ester and go over your daily expectations of her. Ask her what it would take for her to accomplish these things. Clearly the two of you are misaligned with what Ester is supposed to be doing and how much hand-holding she needs.

d. Awkwardly avoid eye contact and make an excuse to kick Ester out of your office. You hate confrontations.

Question 14

You've been feeling pretty overwhelmed at work lately. Not only do you oversee the work of fifteen direct reports, you're also in charge of planning the leadership retreat. One of your employees, Shawn, has been showing up to your office offering to take some work off your hands. You don't know Shawn that well, but he has a reputation as real go-getter. He offers to meet with your newest hires for you, to save you time. What do you do?

a. Tell Shawn thank you and then hand him a to-do list that includes picking up your dry cleaning and your daughter from soccer practice. What you really need is a personal assistant.

b. Let Shawn take *some* tasks off your hands—such as checking people's reports for grammar mistakes—but not the meetings.

c. Tell Shawn to stay in his lane! The thought of handing off work to someone underneath you makes you queasy.

d. Hire Shawn to oversee all the new hires. Plan to meet with him once a month to get some feedback on how everyone is doing. He used to be one of them, so he knows the ropes.

Question 15

Your job is headquartered in Chicago, where you oversee about twenty people. Your boss has been pulling you in a million directions—including sending you to Singapore for two weeks—and upon your return you realize you've lost track of what most of your employees are working on. What's your move?

a. You panic, then reassert your control over everyone. It's important that they remember you're the boss.

b. Do nothing. From your perspective, no news is good news. If people had problems, they would have told you about them.

c. Start with short check-ins with the team to find out what stage everyone is in with their projects. If anyone is at the ready-to-launch stage of a project, now is the time to make sure they get more hands-on guidance.

d. Go to your boss and berate him for putting you in this position. If it wasn't for him, you wouldn't be so out of the loop.

Question 16

Lately you've been forgetting meetings and falling behind on deadlines. One person complained to you that the quarterly report has been sitting on your desk for two months; another that every time she schedules a meeting with you, she stops by to find someone else in your office. They are right—you feel like you're neglecting the people who matter. What do you do?

a. The next time someone comes to you for advice, connect them to someone on your team who can help them out. This way, you help two people connect while saving yourself time.

b. Why is everyone a complainer? You write everyone a long email detailing how busy you are and ask them to please just lay off. You will get to them eventually.

c. Say nothing but complain on social media that your workplace is full of takers. People should learn how to give too.

d. Ask everyone to come up with a list of priorities—what do they care the most about getting feedback on, and what do they care the least about? Work your way through the priority list.

PART 1: SCORING GUIDE

Circle your answer to each question, then add up the total number of circled answers in each column. Note that not all questions have answers in all four categories, and some have more than one answer in a category.

Question Number	Going Through the Motions	Classic Jerk	Conniving Trickster	Ideal Coworker
1	c	a	d	b
2		a	d	b or c
3	c		a or b	d
4		a	b	c or d
5	b	a or d		c
6	a	d	b	c
7		a or c	b	d
8	c	a	d	b
9		a or b	d	c
10	a or d	b		c
11	d	a or b		c
12	c	a	d	b
13	d	a or b		c
14	d	c	a	b

Question Number	Going Through the Motions	Classic Jerk	Conniving Trickster	Ideal Coworker
15	b	a or d		c
16		b	c	a or d
Maximum Score	11	15	11	16
Your Score	_____	_____	_____	_____

GOING THROUGH THE MOTIONS

Your approach to problems at work is hands-off: You don't want to be part of the problem, but you don't want to be part of the solution either. When you feel upset at work, your inclination is to hold it all in. You rarely confront the people who steal your ideas, talk over you, or disrespect you in front of the boss. Groups that are poorly organized won't get any better with you around—you don't see it as your responsibility to get them back on track.

As a boss, you assume that no news is good news. If there were real problems to deal with, someone would have told you. And if someone confronts you with a problem, you shut them down and move on.

People who go through the motions are at risk of becoming neglectful bosses and free riders—the two types of jerks who prefer to disappear when times get tough.

CLASSIC JERK

You follow the profile of a typical jerk at work. If you feel competitive with someone, your inclination is to shoot them down in front of (or directly to) the boss. You take any opportunity that gives you a competitive advantage—including gossiping about your coworkers to smear their reputations or turning two people against each other. You also take advantage of weak bosses who depend on you to get things done, often by demanding an inappropriate amount of control over things.

Classic jerks are the most at risk of becoming bulldozers and micromanagers—the two types of jerks at work who don't hide their naughty behavior behind closed doors. These jerks are often open about their desire to control the people around them.

CONNIVING TRICKSTER

You're a classic jerk at work, taken up a notch or two. When you gossip, you're careful to do so around only those who are one or two steps removed from you to protect your own reputation. You exploit the weakest of bosses, and your dirty behavior is often behind closed doors. If you've made it pretty far, it's probably because you work in an environment that rewards cutthroat behavior.

As a boss, people are probably afraid of you. You likely won't hear about it, but you might see a revolving door of talent and not know why.

Conniving tricksters are most likely to become kiss up/kick downers, credit stealers, and gaslighters—the three types of jerks at work who are masters of disguise—exemplary employees to those with power and bullies to those without it.

IDEAL COWORKER

Even in tough situations, you try to take the perspective of others. When there's conflict at work, you don't run and hide. Instead, you have difficult conversations, even if it means finding out a thing or two about yourself that you don't like.

In groups, you're willing to lead without dominating conversations and agendas. As a boss, you're careful not to fall into micromanagement traps. When you feel overwhelmed you accept help, have your direct reports prioritize work, and figure out what projects need the most attention.

PART 2: ANSWER EXPLANATIONS

Question 1

a. This is classic kiss up/kick down behavior. You might think you're impressing your boss, but you're making a potential enemy out of Gavin in the process.

b. Good choice! It might be awkward to correct Gavin, but at least you're doing it in the least embarrassing way possible.

c. Your gut instinct is probably to avoid looking like a know-it-all, but most people appreciate the feedback if they are doing something clearly wrong.

d. Another example of classic kiss up/kick down behavior. Updating your boss on people's shortcomings shortly after they were hired might raise some red flags—instead of showing the new person support, you're tearing them down behind closed doors.

Question 2

a. This strategy is competitive and unnecessary—a classic tell for a kiss up/kick downer who obsessively compares himself with others.

b. Finding out where you stand relative to the competition is within the normal range of workplace conduct. Rena might not tell you, but it doesn't hurt to ask.

c. A don't ask, don't tell strategy is perfectly appropriate here. Not everyone is comfortable talking about money.

d. Major party foul! This strategy is conniving, the type of thing a well-seasoned kiss up/kick downer would do.

Question 3

a. This is classic bulldozer behavior. Leadership now is critical to getting your way down the road, and you know it.

b. This strategy is a blend of bulldozing and kiss up/kick down. By forcing people to compare themselves with one another, you could be contributing to an unnecessarily competitive group culture.

c. It's perfectly fine to be hands-off about group organization. But be careful with this strategy—if everyone behaved this way nothing would ever get done.

d. Good strategy! You're leading without taking over the agenda of the group.

Question 4

a. This is classic kiss up/kick down behavior. It's not your job to poison the well against Kevin.

b. This move is kiss up/kick down, taken up a few notches. Be careful whom you gossip to—although this strategy can be safer than approaching your boss directly, there's nothing preventing Siena from bringing up your attempt to smear Kevin to the other leaders.

c.   An appropriate strategy in a competitive context like this one.

d.   A hands-off strategy, but an appropriate one.

Question 5

a.   This strategy feels justified, but remember, there are a lot of reasons why groups have a hard time granting credit to the right person. It's better not to assume that the mistake was intentional. Instead, have a conversation about it.

b.   This strategy is too hands-off given the situation. Stewing in resentment will eventually lead you to disengage from work.

c.   This is a great strategy, even if it feels a bit awkward and confrontational. Focus on your perceptions of what happened and ask the group to share their perspectives. By offering solutions, you can prevent the same thing from happening to someone else.

d.   This one is not a great strategy. Approaching Kiera without asking her perspective on what she contributed will probably lead to a long argument and a good deal of awkwardness at the next meeting. It also doesn't prevent credit stealing from happening in the future.

Question 6

a.   It's fine to wait until after the party to deal with Max, but discounting his feelings won't get you anywhere with him. Even if you didn't steal Max's ideas, it's best to talk it out.

Max might not have a lot of power over you now, but he does have the power to tarnish your reputation.

b.   This strategy is very conniving—only the most seasoned credit stealers can pull this one off.

c.   This is a good plan, even if it feels uncomfortable. Make sure you talk about all the invisible labor that you both did. The off-the-radar work is one of the main reasons why people disagree about who should get credit for work.

d.   Like option B, this strategy is quite conniving—and dangerous. You never know who will side with Max.

Question 7

a.   This strategy is rude. Pulling rank to get what you want might work in the short term, but one day Alexander might be *your* boss.

b.   This strategy is the work of someone who really knows how to exploit the boss. It might win you the office, but it could damage your reputation.

c.   Going up the ladder to complain should be done with caution; turning two leaders against each other rarely works out for anyone in the long term.

d.   Good idea! This strategy allows you to ask for what you want (not demand it) and offer something useful in return.

Question 8

a.   It's nice of you to offer to help, but this is classic bulldozer behavior. By blocking anyone from accessing your materials, you've made the team completely reliant on you to get anything done.

b.   Good choice! Training other people is a great first step here. This way, you can use your expertise while also saving yourself time in the future.

c.   This approach is too avoidant. If you're overworked and overburdened, it's fine to turn the job down, but you should suggest a few folks who could replace you on this working group.

d.   This strategy is exploitative bulldozer behavior. Refusing to take the job without complete control over the group is a bit too autocratic.

Question 9

a.   This strategy is a bad idea. Free riding should not beget more free riding; just because your old team did it to you does not mean you should inflict the same punishment on your new team.

b.   Your heart is in the right place but this strategy will likely backfire. Making teams aware of the winners and losers only motivates the top and bottom performers. If your boss took your advice and threatened to take away the bonuses of the bottom performers, you'll wind up with a competitive environment that breeds kiss up/kick down behavior. People will be willing to do anything to climb to the top.

c.   Good strategy! This is what a fairness check is.

d.   This strategy is conniving—especially the "no one needs to know" part. Off-loading work that you pretend to do is classic free rider behavior. Be careful with this approach; it might work in the short term, but eventually word will get out.

Question 10

a. For a boss, this strategy is too hands-off. They might not complain to you, but they will certainly complain about you.

b. This strategy takes care of the temporary problem but signals to employees that mistakes of any kind won't be tolerated. You don't want to create a culture of secrecy where people make mistakes but don't own up to them.

c. Great strategy! Soon you will know who is carrying Irene's load for her so you can address the problem directly.

d. On the surface this strategy makes sense, but it probably won't work long term. Not only does it punish everyone for the bad behavior of one person (which is a quick way to ruin workplace morale) but it probably won't stop Irene from freeloading. Checking in once a month gives Irene ample opportunity to sweet-talk someone into covering her quota.

Question 11

a. The strategy of hovering over people is classic micromanagement. Sometimes we have a hard time letting our old job go, which fuels our desire to micromanage the person who took it over.

b. The strategy of creating too many reporting layers is also classic micromanagement. If Jesse's new leader has very little to do other than oversee Jesse, she might be tempted to micromanage him.

c. Having a conversation about what you both need is a great way to make sure that the two of you are aligned on your goals. The timeline will get you on the same page regarding the speed at which you need work done.

d.   For a manager, this strategy is too hands-off. Immediately turning to your own future goals without spending some time with your team is a sign of a neglectful boss.

Question 12

a.   Sometimes when we can think of nothing for people to do, we have them do arbitrary tasks. It's a sign of micromanagement.

b.   This strategy is a terrific one. It's a good use of time, it's creative, and it will help train people on a skill they rarely get to dedicate hours to.

c.   What a fun boss you are! In all seriousness, this is not a great idea (especially the drinking part). Keep the partying to after work hours.

d.   This strategy is conniving and inappropriate. Don't forget, there's a huge status gap between you and your employees. They might gossip because they feel like they have to, not because they want to.

Question 13

a.   This type of behavior is common among micromanagers. Because Ester did a poor job delivering her criticism, you responded with defensiveness. She will probably respond by stonewalling you—walking away, rolling her eyes, and slamming her office door. Try to stop the cycle of poor communication by clearly articulating why you feel the need to bug her so often and ask her what she needs to get her work done effectively.

b.   This is a very bad strategy. Firing anyone who gives you honest feedback, even if they could work on their delivery, is sending the wrong message. Work on teaching your employees how to deliver criticism more appropriately (the micromanager chapter does just that).

c. Great idea! Finding out where the two of you are misaligned is critical for addressing micromanagement.

d. This strategy is too hands-off for a boss. You can hide from Ester now, but she will probably be back tomorrow with the same issue.

Question 14

a. This strategy is exploitative, and it won't help Shawn's career. You're taking advantage of someone who thinks granting a favor will get him a raise. It never does—only performing well at work does.

b. Great idea! Make sure the tasks are useful and you have careful oversight of his work.

c. This strategy certainly does not scale. The art of being a good manager is knowing when to accept help. If you keep this up, you will burn out.

d. This strategy is risky. If Shawn is a kiss up/kick downer, you're giving him the perfect opportunity to control the reputation of the people he works with.

Question 15

a. The pattern of long periods of neglect followed by control is classic neglectful boss behavior.

b. This strategy is too hands-off for a boss. Don't assume that if no one is complaining, everyone is fine. There are a lot of reasons why people don't complain to neglectful bosses—the first being that they think they will be ignored if they do.

c.   Good strategy! Most people want the most attention right before they launch. Knowing who needs the most help right now can help you prioritize.

d.   It always feels good to play the blame game, but complaining up won't solve the problem. Address the problem with your boss but be careful in how you criticize (the chapters on the micromanager and neglectful boss offer some guidelines).

Question 16

a.   Good plan! Off-loading the work of time thieves to your team is a great way to help them form connections (just be careful that the work is worthwhile).

b.   This strategy makes you feel good in the moment, but the time you spent constructing your woe-is-me email could have been spent editing that report. It also doesn't help you solve the underlying problem—that you don't seem to have enough time for the people who matter the most.

c.   Blasting your coworkers on social media is never a good idea. According to a CareerBuilder survey, about 70 percent of employers use social media to screen candidates, and about a third have either fired or reprimanded someone because they didn't approve of their online behavior. Blasting your current employer could cost you your job.

d.   Another good plan! Getting people to prioritize is key to getting yourself back on track if you're trending toward neglect.

Quiz 2

Am I an Effective Ally?

Most of us have experienced jerks at work not only as victims but as observers. This quiz will help you assess how you respond to jerks when someone other than yourself is the target. The goal is to find out whether you're an effective ally and, if not, what type of not-so-supportive coworker you are—virtue signaler, dramatic savior, or actionless observer.

Just like the "Am I a Jerk at Work?" quiz, this one has two parts. In part 1, you will answer ten questions. At the end, I will show you how to score your quiz and describe each of the four ally types. In part 2, I provide an answer guide where I walk through my logic in placing your answer into the category I did.

One of my favorite ways of taking this quiz is having multiple people answer the questions from my perspective. What type of ally do other people think I am, and do their answers jive with how I see myself? Are there some people who see me as an effective ally and others who think of me more as an actionless observer? I've learned a ton about myself by asking other people what they think I would do in different social situations, and I bet you will too.

Enjoy!

Question 1

Your boss has been feeling overwhelmed lately. To cope, she started handing off her one-on-one meetings with new employees to Steve— an experienced coworker who knows how to navigate the office. However, Steve has a dark side—he's willing to do anything to get ahead, including trash-talking whomever he sees as competition. You and Steve stay out of each other's way, and he doesn't have a problem with you. What's your move?

a. Ignore Steve and whatever drama he creates with the new employees. This problem doesn't concern you.

b. Post about the problem on the company's internal communication platform. You leave out names and specifics but declare your support for everyone who has ever been bullied at work.

c. Express your concerns privately to the boss, emphasizing how important it was for you to have direct communication with her when you first started, even if it's just for fifteen minutes a week.

d. Pull Steve aside and warn him. One wrong move and you'll blast his embarrassing pictures from last year's Halloween party over the company listserv.

Question 2

As a manager at an ice cream company, you oversee a team of twelve whose job is to come up with a new flavor of ice cream. About a month in, your newest team member, Mona, complains to you that Tyler—one of the team's long-standing members—has stolen her idea for boozy vanilla fudge and claimed it as his own. Tyler scoffs at the accusation, claiming that Mona came up only with vanilla and he filled in the rest. What's your response?

a. Sit down with Tyler, Mona, and the rest of the team and talk about the importance of keeping track of contributions. Clearly this team has some communication issues, and they might need to move to a more formal process of documenting who did what.

b. Tell them both that you don't have time for petty bickering.

c. Send the team a long email about how important it is that they support one another and value one another's hard work. There is no "I" in "team," people!

d. Call a team meeting and chastise Tyler for bullying a junior person. He's been here for a long time; he should know better.

Question 3

Lately in meetings, your coworker Adam has been talking for about 50 percent of the time, despite being one of ten people. Adam doesn't seem to have much of an agenda, and no one seems motivated to interrupt him. What do you do?

a. Interrupt Adam, tell him that you're tired of the sound of his voice and you're pretty sure everyone else is too.

b. Nothing. This meeting will be over soon anyway.

c. Do nothing in the moment but approach a few people after the meeting and come up with a plan of what you will do next time Adam takes over. You recommend putting one person in charge of calling on people who haven't had a chance to speak yet.

d. Announce the need for a town hall where everyone discusses their feelings about people who take over meetings.

Question 4

You work for a company that wants to hire Min-sun—a top analyst at her current company. Min-sun is so talented your company is willing to pay the big bucks just to stop her from working for the competition. What do you think is the best strategy moving forward?

a. Do whatever it takes to hire her and don't worry about what comes next. The important thing is getting her off the job market.

b. Hire her and put some steps in place to evaluate her performance every six months. If she refuses to be evaluated, that's a big red flag.

c. Hire her and then place her on a team of go-getters. Do interviews with the team to make sure she's working as hard as everyone else. And if she isn't, you can lecture her in front of the team.

d. Hire her and make her brand ambassador. Who cares if she does any work—she has the perfect look to represent your company's values.

Question 5

You're on a team with five other people working under a tight deadline, and meetings feel like chaos. People sit around a table yelling ideas into the air, and one person stands at the front of the room jotting things down on the whiteboard. At the end of the last meeting, your coworker Stan complained to you that no matter how many good ideas he has, they never get written on the whiteboard. To prevent this from happening in the future, you:

a. Suggest to the team that you pause every twenty minutes and take stock of what ideas have been generated and who came up with them. Have one person take notes each meeting to keep a record. Keep the role rotating, so no one person feels the burden.

b. Open the next meeting with a lecture on how everyone needs to pay attention to Stan more. He's feeling ignored and that's not okay.

c. Tell Stan that if he wants to have his voice heard, he needs to stand up for himself. It's not your job to make sure his ideas land on the whiteboard.

d. At the next company party, announce the importance of having all voices heard. It's not until six months from now, but this issue can wait.

Question 6

Nathaniel has not been pulling his weight on your team. One day, he shows up with work that is so poorly done that it seems like his new intern did it. Later that day, you overhear someone crying in the bathroom. It's Nathaniel's new intern, Winnie, and she's so overwhelmed by Nathaniel's inappropriate work requests she doesn't know what to do. What's your move?

a. Find a new bathroom. You hate workplace drama.

b. Give Winnie a big hug and offer to take her out for drinks at the end of the day. You're happy to be a shoulder to cry on, but you have no plans to interfere. Nathaniel's intern is Nathaniel's business.

c. Pull Nathaniel aside and ask why he's off-loading his work to Winnie. Tell him that you're happy to meet with the team to come up with a plan of getting him back on track, but you're concerned Winnie is overwhelmed by picking up his slack.

d. Drag Winnie into the next team meeting and have her share her experience. Make sure you stand up there with her and offer your support moving forward.

Question 7

Marshall is one of your closest friends at work. You have different bosses, but the two of you frequently go to each other for advice. But lately, Marshall has been very withdrawn. You stop by his office to see if he's okay, and you overhear his boss telling him that the work they're doing together is confidential and if he tells anyone about it, both of their careers would be in jeopardy. You find this odd, given how collaborative Marshall's boss used to be. How do you respond?

a. Approach Marshall and tell him that you miss connecting with him and you're concerned about his relationship with his boss. Don't pressure him to tell you what's happening; instead, come prepared with a list of people he can talk with about his issues, confidentially.

b. Walk backward very quietly and return to your office. This conversation was clearly meant to be private.

c. Immediately email your boss and your boss's boss (for good measure) to express your concerns that Marshall is being abused. Tell them everything you overheard.

d. Start an Employees Against Isolation and Abuse interest group. Invite Marshall to join. If he wants, he can share his story.

Question 8

Your coworker Finn seems totally exhausted. His boss is constantly hovering over him, micromanaging his every move. Finn works more hours than anyone else but he's missed the last three major deadlines. He asks you for advice on how to deal with a micromanager. What do you tell him?

a. Tell him to hide, shut off his office lights and pretend not to be there. Eventually his boss will move on to a new target.

b. Recommend he approach his boss for a chat. Remind him that leading with micromanagement might make her defensive; a better strategy is to start a conversation about big-picture goals. Recommend that he not only share his goals but ask her what her goals are. They might be misaligned on what he's supposed to be doing at work.

c. Tell him that he should bring his true self to work. And this means telling his boss how he feels, no matter how resistant she is.

d. Find everyone else who reports to Finn's boss and interview them. You want to find out how widespread this micromanagement problem is before you bring it up with the top leaders of the organization.

Question 9

You and your coworker Morgan started working for the same company about five months ago and you have different bosses. Your boss mentors and trains you, but Morgan's boss is never around. In fact, Morgan has met with her boss only once since she started, and she's struggling to find her place at work. What's the best way to respond to Morgan's request for help?

    a.   Give Morgan advice on how to get her boss's attention. She should start small by asking her boss for a thirty-minute meeting in the next few weeks. Come prepared with a handful of asks (no more than three) that she needs help with right now. The key to handling neglectful bosses is not to overwhelm them with requests.

    b.   Skip giving Morgan advice and go directly to your boss to ask if Morgan can get transferred to your team.

    c.   Buy Morgan a bunch of self-help books on taking her life back. Photograph her reading them and then post them on your social media account with lots of clever hashtags that signal how awesome Morgan is.

    d.   You can't control Morgan's boss, so you're not sure what she wants from you. If you were in her position, you'd be looking for a new job.

Question 10

You've been working with your boss for several years, and you have a great relationship. His mentorship is superb, and you've quickly risen through the ranks at work. But lately, word of his skills has spread a little too far and wide, and he spends most of his day helping random people who are looking for advice on how to get ahead. He's exhausted and overwhelmed and doesn't have much time for anyone on his team. Your new coworker, Janelle, complains to you that she's not getting the same level of mentorship you got. How do you handle the situation?

a. Tweet about what a generous boss you have and make sure you tag him in it. Then complain about him behind his back.

b. Ask your boss if you can help mentor any of these random people who stop by. It would free up his time (so he has more of it for Janelle) and would help you form new connections and hone your mentorship skills.

c. Find all the people who keep bugging your boss, go to their offices, and tell them to bug someone else. Surely your boss will appreciate you intervening on his behalf.

d. Tell Janelle there's nothing she can do. Your boss can choose to spend his time however he wants.

PART 1: SCORING GUIDE

Circle your answer to each question, then add up the total number of circled answers in each column.

Question Number	Virtue Signaler	Dramatic Savior	Actionless Observer	Effective Ally
1	b	d	a	c
2	c	d	b	a
3	d	a	b	c
4	d	c	a	b
5	d	b	c	a

Question Number	Virtue Signaler	Dramatic Savior	Actionless Observer	Effective Ally
6	b	d	a	c
7	d	c	b	a
8	c	d	a	b
9	c	b	d	a
10	a	c	d	b
Maximum Score	10	10	10	10
Your Score	_____	_____	_____	_____

VIRTUE SIGNALER

Your actions have the appearance of helping, but they do little to move the needle on how people behave at work. You prefer public declarations of support—think speeches at company parties and posts on social media—especially in workplaces where showing support is the normative thing to do.

If you witness jerk-at-work behavior firsthand, you turn the other cheek. The drama that comes along with getting involved isn't worth it to you, especially if intervening could cost you social capital. Newcomers at work initially misread you; they see your public support as a sign that you will also support them in private. But you don't, making you a dangerous faux ally.

DRAMATIC SAVIOR

Your heart is in the right place, my friend, but your rescue missions are a tad dramatic. You have no problem stepping in to help a victim, even in public settings. You prefer grand gestures of support, followed by quick-witted insults meant to shame and humiliate the offender.

We all love watching a jerk get a taste of their own medicine, but your methods can fuel the fire of conflict. Victims who feel uncertain about where they stand appreciate your protective behavior, but they might also feel isolated by it. Some aren't ready to open up, and at times, they feel pressured by you to do so. Because of your tactics, the victims you aim to protect can wind up with only one friend at work: you.

ACTIONLESS OBSERVER

The way you see it, if you're not part of the problem, you don't need to be part of the solution. Other people's jerk-at-work problems are not yours to solve. You figure that if you had to learn how to navigate around difficult people at work, so too should everyone else. On teams, you often let free riders and bulldozers take advantage of coworkers; if it were that important, someone else would step in to help. When you witness people being victimized by bad bosses, you might give them a piece of advice, but you rarely speak up on their behalf.

In some cases, your avoidance stems from conflict aversion—perhaps you feel unsure at work and the last thing you want to do is rock the boat. In others, it stems from feeling overworked—you're stretched so thin at work you can't find time to intervene for someone else.

EFFECTIVE ALLY

You respond to jerk-at-work behavior with a combination of appropriate confrontation and advice giving. You realize that the solution to jerks at work is to form allies at work, and you're quick to help victims find the right people to buffer and protect them. Grand public gestures of support are not your style. If confrontation is called for, you prefer one-on-one meetings. You realize that public shaming rarely gets you to where you want to be. Instead, you use tactics aimed at reducing conflict rather than exacerbating it. You prefer open and honest communication between those who are involved as an initial strategy.

Often you find yourself in a mediator role, helping two people with conflict work it out. Bosses love having you around because you know how to ease interpersonal tensions without creating the appearance of taking sides. If you aren't a leader already, there's a good chance you will be someday.

PART 2: ANSWER EXPLANATIONS

Question 1

    a.   It might seem wise not to get involved in a problem that doesn't concern you, but in this case, your decision might come back to haunt you. Bosses who rely on a kiss up/kick downer once will probably do it again.

    b.   Criticizing people on communication platforms at work is rarely a good idea. Most people will spend their time gossiping about whom they think you were referring to rather than on developing actionable solutions to the problem.

c. It's hard to know when to get involved in a problem that doesn't concern you without looking like you're meddling. This approach does just that. It allows you to raise concerns with the boss without trash-talking Steve. Nice choice!

d. Blackmail rarely works to change how people behave at work. Once the threat disappears, the bad behavior returns. I doubt there are enough bad pictures of Steve to sustain this approach.

Question 2

a. Great solution! Accusations of credit stealing are common at work; teaching your team how to sort out contributions early will save you a ton of time down the road.

b. It's often tempting to tell your team to handle their own conflict, but this strategy works only if the team has the skills to do so. In this case, Tyler will probably get credit for the flavor simply because he's more senior. Clearly this team needs a bit of guidance.

c. This minimal effort approach says to your team, "I care enough to mention it but not enough to help solve it."

d. The next time Tyler shows up at work, he will probably cross his arms and refuse to contribute anything. Chastising people publicly usually leads to disengagement at work.

Question 3

a. This harsh approach might shut down Adam right now, but it also (inadvertently) discourages anyone else from speaking up in meetings for fear of being humiliated by you. New employees and those who don't feel like they have a voice will be terrified to contribute when you're around.

b. True, but you will waste hours, if not days, of your life if you continue to let Adam dominate meetings.

c. This behind-the-scenes approach tackles the problem without making a fool out of Adam. You also have a plan for encouraging new voices to speak up, solving two problems at once.

d. Creating town halls because of one person's bad behavior at work creates the illusion of a widespread problem. It also wastes a lot of people's time.

Question 4

a. As temping as this strategy may be, it will probably backfire. With no system of accountability in place, Min-sun has no reason to stay motivated once she's hired.

b. Great idea. Falling in love with superstars is dangerous business. Putting at least one step in place to ensure that Min-sun lives up to her expectations is smart. It also gives you a way out if she doesn't.

c. Your team of go-getters will be so intimidated by Min-sun, I doubt they would tell on her. Besides, most employees don't want to throw the team superstar under the bus.

d. This strategy is classic virtue signaling. Min-sun has skills—don't forget that! Chances are, everyone at your organization is eager to see those skills in action.

Question 5

a. Sometimes chaotic meetings are unavoidable. This strategy forces everyone to slow down and make sure the group is on the same page. People like Stan who are uncomfortable yelling over everyone can use these moments to share with the team how they feel. The team can recalibrate and re-think their strategy of making sure all voices are heard.

b. Poor Stan! You thought he felt awkward trying to contrib-ute before; imagine how he feels now that you called him out. The result will be fewer contributions from Stan, not more.

c. A lot of people are uncomfortable interrupting others to get their ideas onto the whiteboard. This strategy discourages anyone who isn't loud and domineering from contributing to group discussions.

d. This plan is too little too late. It's also vague and unaction-able and clearly not tethered to a specific problem.

Question 6

a. I understand the temptation to do your business in peace, but keep in mind that this might be your one chance to find out why Nathaniel is off-loading his work to someone not qualified to do it. It's not just Winnie who suffers from Nathaniel's behavior; your whole team might too.

b. Winnie will probably assume that you have her back, and she's right to think so. Your behavior is misleading and un-fair to Winnie. She needs real allies, not people who pre-tend to care.

c. Talking to Nathaniel in private is the right approach here. People off-load work for all sorts of reasons, some of which they might not be comfortable discussing with the whole team. Being focused on solutions should also help Nathan-iel avoid the urge to defend himself.

d. As a new person at work with very little status, the last thing Winnie needs is to report her boss to a bunch of strangers. This strategy will probably lead to Winnie's resignation.

Question 7

a. This approach is perfect for handling a delicate issue like this one. You communicated your concerns to Marshall without pressuring him to open up to you. People in Marshall's situation often feel so overwhelmed by their mistreatment at work, the last thing they want to figure out is whom to go to for help. It's great that you did the legwork for him.

b. Yes, it is the case that Marshall's boss intended for this conversation to be private. But it raised major red flags, so it's worth it to (delicately) bring the issue up to Marshall. If you misunderstood what was happening, no harm done.

c. I suggest you slow down and think this one through before you immediately pull the alarm on Marshall's boss. If Marshall is being manipulated to do unethical things, then the truth will need to come out slowly, and steps will need to be put in place to protect Marshall.

d. This virtue-signaling strategy does little else than raise awareness of an issue that might affect very few people in your organization. If Marshall is being gaslit by his boss, I doubt he would join your group. He might not be at the stage of admitting there's a problem, let alone talking with a group of coworkers about it.

Question 8

a. Hiding is a temporary solution to the problem of being micromanaged. What will happen when Finn needs to eat or use the bathroom?

b. The last thing most people want to do when they're being micromanaged is spend more time with the boss, but you do a great job of selling it. One of the main reasons why people feel micromanaged is because their boss thinks they were hired for one reason and they think they were hired for another. Aligning goals can help solve this miscommunication problem.

c. I understand the urge to unload on bad bosses, but it rarely changes their behavior. Radical candor here won't get Finn to where he needs to be. His boss will probably justify her behavior then kick him out of her office.

d. It is not your place to interview everyone Finn works with. He didn't give you permission to share his concerns with others at work, and who knows which of these employees will go straight to Finn's boss to report his complaint. Finn needs to handle his issue directly, not via the gossip network.

Question 9

a. Great advice for roping in a neglectful boss. Most of us are tempted to make an emergency ask, but by offering up a two-week time frame, Morgan is more likely to get a response from her boss. Busy bosses who are already tempted to neglect don't have time for our "emergencies."

b. A strange move for someone at the same level as Morgan; these types of moves are usually orchestrated by higher-ups.

If you would like Morgan on your team, talk to her about it first. Don't assume you know she wants to give up on her boss completely.

c. It's nice of you to buy Morgan books, but her time is better spent tackling her boss problem head-on.

d. This no-effort approach will surely make Morgan feel helpless at work. Morgan shouldn't give up until she's tried to engage her boss and failed.

Question 10

a. Having an online persona that contradicts your in-person persona is in the air these days. Most people at work don't like it.

b. This approach will save your boss time and give you some experience in training newcomers at work. Great strategy.

c. You might want to ask your boss first before you make yourself his bodyguard. He may enjoy mentoring these people—and it's not your place to block them.

d. Despite having a wealth of knowledge of how to make things work with your boss, you're not willing to share it. Janelle will quickly learn to find new allies in the office.

NOTES

Introduction

14 **A surprising 70 percent**: Lindsay Kolowich Cox, "Eleven reasons having friends at work makes you happier," *Hubspot*, February 1, 2017, https://blog.hubspot.com/marketing/workplace-friendships.

1: Kiss Up/Kick Downer

19 **There's a personality trait**: Cynthia Kay Stevens and Amy L. Kristof, "Making the right impression: A field study of applicant impression management during job interviews," *Journal of Applied Psychology* 80, no. 5 (1995), https://doi.org/10.1037/0021-9010.80.5.587.

21 **In a study, Siyu**: Siyu Yu, Gavin J. Kilduff, and Tessa V. West, "Status Acuity: How the Ability to Accurately Perceive Status Hierarchies Reduces Status Conflict and Benefits Team Performance" (Unpublished manuscript, 2021).

22 **In a recent Mercer survey**: Mercer, "Connectivity in the human age: Global Talent Trends 2019," www.mercer.com/our-thinking/career/global-talent-hr-trends-infographics.html.

23 **Believe it or not**: Felicia Pratto et al., "Social dominance orientation: A personality variable predicting social and political attitudes," *Journal of Personality and Social Psychology* 67, no. 4 (1994), https://doi.org/10.1037/0022-3514.67.4.741.

23 **Kiss up/kick downers quickly figure out**: Sanne Feenstra et al., "The Hazard of Teetering at the Top and Being Tied to the Bottom: The Interactive Relationship of Power, Stability, and Social Dominance Orientation with Work Stress," *Applied Psychology* 66, no. 4 (2017), https://doi.org/10.1111/apps.12104.

25 **From then on**: Katherine R. Thorson, Oana D. Dumitru, and Tessa V. West, "Physiological linkage among successful high-status women in international teams," *Social Cognitive and Affective Neuroscience* 16, nos. 1–2 (2021), https://doi.org/10.1093/scan/nsaa112.

27 **Once they met**: Tessa V. West et al., "A little similarity goes a long way: The effects of peripheral but self-revealing similarities on improving and sustaining interracial relationships," *Journal of Personality and Social Psychology* 107, no. 1 (2014), https://doi.org/10.1037/a0036556.

27 **The National Football League's**: NFL, "NFL Junior Rotation Program Overview," www.nfl.com/careers/jrp.

28 **Bosses can be the victims**: Daniel C. Feldman, "Toxic Mentors or Toxic Proteges? A Critical Re-Examination of Dysfunctional Mentoring," *Human Resource Management Review* 9, no. 3 (September 1999), https://doi.org/10.1016/S1053-4822(99)00021-2.

30 **The farther away**: Sarah P. Doyle et al., "Helping Others Most When They Are Not Too Close: Status Distance as a Determinant of Interpersonal Helping in Organizations," *Academy of Management Discoveries* 2, no. 2 (2016), https://doi.org/10.5465/amd.2014.0104.

34 **My research has found**: Tessa V. West, Adam R. Pearson, and Chadly Stern, "Anxiety perseverance in intergroup interaction: When incidental explanations backfire," *Journal of Personality and Social Psychology* 107, no. 5 (2014), https://doi.org/10.1037/a0037941.

2: The Credit Stealer

41 **Credit stealing is one:** Leigh Thompson and George Loewenstein, "Egocentric interpretations of fairness and interpersonal conflict," *Organizational Behavior and Human Decision Processes* 51, no. 2 (March 1992), https://doi.org/10.1016/0749-5978(92)90010-5.

41 **A surprising 25 percent:** Chrome River, "Chrome River survey reveals insights on business travel expense fraud, how businesses can deter it," May 31, 2018, www.chromeriver.com/news/chrome-river-survey-reveals -insights-on-business-travel-expense-fraud.

41 **About half of people:** Lou Solomon, "The Top Complaints from Employees About Their Leaders," *Harvard Business Review*, June 24, 2015, https://hbr .org/2015/06/the-top-complaints-from-employees-about-their-leaders.

44 **Male flies that pirate:** Randy Thornhill, "Adaptive Female-Mimicking Behavior in a Scorpionfly," *Science* 205, no. 4404 (1979), https://doi.org /10.1126/science.205.4404.412.

45 **According to UC Berkeley's:** Daniel H. Stein et al., "The Mistaken Preference for Overclaiming Credit in Groups" (Unpublished manuscript, January 6, 2020).

49 **In the largest study:** Taeya M. Howell et al., "Who gets credit for input? Demographic and structural status cues in voice recognition," *Journal of Applied Psychology* 100, no. 6 (2015), https://doi.org/10.1037/apl0000025.

49 **The best predictor:** Raymond T. Sparrowe et al., "Social networks and the performance of individuals and groups," *Academy of Management Journal* 44, no. 2 (2001), https://doi.org/10.2307/3069458.

50 **They may already be:** Steven R. Corman and Craig R. Scott, "Perceived Networks, Activity Foci, and Observable Communication in Social Collectives," *Communication Theory* 4, no. 3 (2006), https://doi.org/10.1111/j.1468 -2885.1994.tb00089.x; Miller McPherson, Lynn Smith-Lovin, and James M. Cook, "Birds of a Feather: Homophily in Social Networks," *Annual Review of Sociology* 27, no. 1 (2001), https://doi.org/10.1146/annurev.soc.27.1.415.

50 **A little prosociality:** Mark C. Bolino and Adam M. Grant, "The Bright Side of Being Prosocial at Work, and the Dark Side, Too: A Review and Agenda for Research on Other-Oriented Motives, Behavior, and Impact in

Organizations," *Academy of Management Annals* 10, no. 1 (2016), https://doi
.org/10.5465/19416520.2016.1153260.

51 **When people speak up:** Elizabeth J. McClean et al., "The Social Consequences of Voice: An Examination of Voice Type and Gender on Status
and Subsequent Leader Emergence," *Academy of Management Journal* 61,
no. 5 (2018), https://doi.org/10.5465/amj.2016.0148.

55 **Diverse teams come up with:** Samuel R. Sommers, "On racial diversity
and group decision making: Identifying multiple effects of racial composition on jury deliberations," *Journal of Personality and Social Psychology* 90,
no. 4 (2006), https://doi.org/10.1037/0022-3514.90.4.597.

58 **You experienced the:** Thomas Gilovich, Justin Kruger, and Victoria
Husted Medvec, "The Spotlight Effect Revisited: Overestimating the Mani-
fest Variability of Our Actions and Appearance," *Journal of Experimental
Social Psychology* 38, no. 1 (January 2002), https://doi.org/10.1006/jesp.2001
.1490.

59 **But I don't think:** Emily Pronin et al., "Everyday magical powers: The role
of apparent mental causation in the overestimation of personal influence,"
Journal of Personality and Social Psychology 91, no. 2 (2006), https://doi.org
/10.1037/0022-3514.91.2.218.

63 **Take, for example:** Seale Harris, *Banting's Miracle: The Story of the Discovery of Insulin* (Philadelphia: Lippincott, 1946).

64 **According to Banting's recall:** Louis Rosenfeld, "Insulin: Discovery and
Controversy," *Clinical Chemistry* 48, no. 12 (2002), https://doi.org/10.1093
/clinchem/48.12.2270.

64 **Decades later, Karolinska Institute:** Nicholas Wade, "Nobel Follies," *Science* 211, no. 4489 (1981), https://doi.org/10.1126/science.211.4489.1404.

3: The Bulldozer

74 **Usually, power is based:** Cameron Anderson and Robb Willer, "Do Status
Hierarchies Benefit Groups? A Bounded Functionalist Account of Status," in *The Psychology of Social Status*, ed. Joey T. Cheng, Jessica L. Tracy,
and Cameron Anderson (New York: Springer, 2014).

79 **I like to follow**: Mark Goulston, "How to know if you talk too much," *Harvard Business Review*, June 3, 2015, https://hbr.org/2015/06/how-to-know-if-you-talk-too-much.

80 **In my research, we found**: Katherine R. Thorson, Oana D. Dumitru, and Tessa V. West, "Physiological linkage among successful high-status women in international teams," *Social Cognitive and Affective Neuroscience* 16, nos. 1–2 (2021), https://doi.org/10.1093/scan/nsaa112.

80 **other research has confirmed this**: Dana R. Carney, "The nonverbal expression of power, status, and dominance," *Current Opinion in Psychology* 33 (June 2020), https://doi.org/10.1016/j.copsyc.2019.12.004.

84 **For some, the threat**: Matthew Feinberg, Robb Willer, and Michael Schultz, "Gossip and Ostracism Promote Cooperation in Groups," *Psychological Science* 25, no. 3 (2014), https://doi.org/10.1177/0956797613510184.

4: The Free Rider

91 **Three or four oxen**: David A. Kravitz and Barbara Martin, "Ringelmann rediscovered: The original article," *Journal of Personality and Social Psychology* 50, no. 5 (1986), https://doi.org/10.1037/0022-3514.50.5.936.

94 **Conscientiousness is one**: Ian J. Deary et al., "More Intelligent, More Dependable Children Live Longer: A 55-Year Longitudinal Study of a Representative Sample of the Scottish Nation," *Psychological Science* 19, no. 9 (2008), https://doi.org/10.1111/j.1467-9280.2008.02171.x.

94 **They are reliable**: Avan Jassawalla, Hemant Sashittal, and Avinash Sashittal, "Students' Perceptions of Social Loafing: Its Antecedents and Consequences in Undergraduate Business Classroom Teams," *Academy of Management Learning & Education* 8, no. 1 (2009), https://doi.org/10.5465/amle.2009.37012178.

94 **Conscientious team members**: Michaéla C. Schippers, "Social Loafing Tendencies and Team Performance: The Compensating Effect of Agreeableness and Conscientiousness," *Academy of Management Learning & Education* 13, no. 1 (2014), https://doi.org/10.5465/amle.2012.0191.

96 **At work, cohesion usually**: Robert C. Liden et al., "Social Loafing: A Field Investigation," *Journal of Management* 30, no. 2 (2004), https://doi.org/10.1016/j.jm.2003.02.002.

96 **In fact, between 10 and 20 percent**: Michael J. Rosenfeld, Reuben J. Thomas, and Sonia Hausen, "Disintermediating your friends: How online dating in the United States displaces other ways of meeting," *Proceedings of the National Academy of Sciences* 116, no. 36 (2019), https://doi.org/10.1073/pnas.1908630116.

96 **We can also easily**: Chris Lam, "The Role of Communication and Cohesion in Reducing Social Loafing in Group Projects," *Business and Professional Communication Quarterly* 78, no. 4 (2015), https://doi.org/10.1177/2329490615596417.

97 **Caroline reminds me**: Vasyl Taras et al., "Straight from the horse's mouth: Justifications and prevention strategies provided by free riders on global virtual teams," *Journal of Management and Training for Industries* 5, no. 3 (2018), https://search.informit.org/doi/10.3316/informit.170441492915342.

98 **In fact, more than half**: Anthony J. Nyberg et al., "Collective Pay for Performance: A Cross-Disciplinary Review and Meta-Analysis," *Journal of Management* 44, no. 6 (April 2018), https://doi.org/10.1177/0149206318770732.

98 **The worst version of this**: Matt Bolch, "Rewarding the Team: It requires careful consideration to craft a compensation plan that encourages and rewards employees for effective teamwork," *HR Magazine* 52, no. 2 (February 2007).

98 **You lose what social scientists**: Kipling Williams, Stephen G. Harkins, and Bibb Latané, "Identifiability as a deterrant to social loafing: Two cheering experiments," *Journal of Personality and Social Psychology* 40, no. 2 (1981), https://doi.org/10.1037/0022-3514.40.2.303.

99 **This is a dangerous move**: Jennifer M. George, "Extrinsic and Intrinsic Origins of Perceived Social Loafing in Organizations," *Academy of Management Journal* 35, no. 1 (1992), https://doi.org/10.5465/256478.

100 **Most teams fall into**: Steve W. J. Kozlowski and Daniel R. Ilgen, "Enhancing the Effectiveness of Work Groups and Teams," *Psychological Science in the Public Interest* 7, no. 3 (2006), https://doi.org/10.1111/j.1529-1006.2006.00030.x.

100 **As one engineer**: Mary-Ann Russon, "How to get paid for doing nothing: Inside Silicon Valley's controversial 'rest and vest' culture," *International Business Times* August 7, 2017, www.ibtimes.co.uk/how-get-paid-doing -nothing-inside-silicon-valleys-controversial-rest-vest-culture-1633884.

101–102 **Across different types of teams**: Robert B. Lount, Jr., et al., "Only When Others Are Watching: The Contingent Efforts of High Status Group Members," *Management Science* 65, no. 7 (2019), https://doi.org/10.1287/mnsc .2018.3103.

104 **Fairness is a minimum requirement**: Kenneth H. Price, David A. Harrison, and Joanne H. Gavin, "Withholding inputs in team contexts: Member composition, interaction processes, evaluation structure, and social loafing," *Journal of Applied Psychology* 91, no. 6 (2006), https://doi.org/10.1037 /0021-9010.91.6.1375.

106 **Michigan State Broad College of Business**: Christy Zhou Koval et al., "The burden of responsibility: Interpersonal costs of high self-control," *Journal of Personality and Social Psychology* 108, no. 5 (2015), https://doi.org /10.1037/pspi0000015.

108 **Professor of economics**: David Gill et al., "First-Place Loving and Last-Place Loathing: How Rank in the Distribution of Performance Affects Effort Provision," *Management Science* 65, no. 2 (2019), https://doi.org/10.1287 /mnsc.2017.2907.

109 **Animal researchers first observed**: Allen J. Neuringer, "Animals Respond for Food in the Presence of Free Food," *Science* 166, no. 3903 (1969), https://doi.org/10.1126/science.166.3903.399.

109 **People do it too**: Robert D. Tarte, "Contrafreeloading in Humans," *Psychological Reports* 49, no. 3 (1981), https://doi.org/10.2466/pr0.1981.49.3.859.

111 **No, this isn't a religion**: N. T. Feather, "Protestant Ethic, conservatism, and values," *Journal of Personality and Social Psychology* 46, no. 5 (1984), https://doi.org/10.1037/0022-3514.46.5.1132.

5: The Micromanager

121 **About 79 percent**: Harry E. Chambers, *My Way or the Highway: Micromanagement Survival Guide* (San Francisco: Berrett-Koehler Publishers, 2004).

121 **Eighty-nine percent of bosses**: David Sturt and Todd Nordstrom, "10 shocking workplace stats you need to know," *Forbes,* March 8, 2018, www .forbes.com/sites/davidsturt/2018/03/08/10-shocking-workplace-stats -you-need-to-know/?sh=42e412c2f3af.

121 **Above the water**: Richard D. White, "The Micromanagement Disease: Symptoms, Diagnosis, and Cure," *Public Personnel Management* 39, no. 1 (2010), https://doi.org/10.1177/009102601003900105.

124 **Fast, high-quality decision-making**: Iskandar Aminov, Aaron De Smet, Gregor Jost, and David Mendelsohn, "Decision making in the age of urgency," McKinsey & Company, survey, April 30, 2019, www.mckinsey.com /business-functions/organization/our-insights/decision-making-in-the-age -of-urgency.

124 **Micromanagers are strong believers**: Jeffrey Pfeffer et al., "Faith in Supervision and the Self-Enhancement Bias: Two Psychological Reasons Why Managers Don't Empower Workers," *Basic and Applied Social Psychology* 20, no. 4 (December 1, 1998), https://doi.org/10.1207/s15324834basp2004_8.

125 **Most managers are promoted**: White, "The Micromanagement Disease."

125 **Bill Gates, Jeff Bezos**: Mike Ramsey, "Electric-car pioneer Elon Musk charges head-on in Detroit," *The Wall Street Journal,* January 11, 2015, www.wsj.com/articles/electric-car-pioneer-elon-musk-charges-head -on-at-detroit-1421033527.

125 **It's no wonder that in a survey**: Aminov, De Smet, Jost, and Mendelsohn, "Decision making."

128 **"on your own." "Set boundaries"**: Matt Villano, "The control freak in the corner office," *The New York Times,* May 28, 2006, www.nytimes.com/2006 /05/28/business/yourmoney/28advi.html; Ben Wigert and Ryan Pendell, "The ultimate guide to micromanagers: Signs, causes, solutions," Gallup, July 17, 2020, www.gallup.com/workplace/315530/ultimate-guide-micro managers-signs-causes-solutions.aspx.

130 **"Too much nagging"**: Menelaos Apostolou and Yan Wang, "The Challenges of Keeping an Intimate Relationship: An Evolutionary Examination," *Evolutionary Psychology* 18, no. 3 (2020), https://doi.org/10.1177/1474704 920953526.

131 **Karen and Matt's interaction:** John M. Gottman, "Repair and the core triad of balance," in *The Marriage Clinic: A Scientifically-Based Marital Therapy* (New York: W. W. Norton & Company, 1999).

133 **In Gottman's studies:** John M. Gottman, *The Seven Principles for Making Marriage Work* (New York: Crown, 1999).

135 **This pattern is common:** Kathleen A. Eldridge et al., "Demand-withdraw communication in severely distressed, moderately distressed, and non-distressed couples: Rigidity and polarity during relationship and personal problem discussions," *Journal of Family Psychology* 21, no. 2 (2007), https://doi.org/10.1037/0893-3200.21.2.218.

135 **In fact, 51 percent:** Annamarie Mann, "What are the best employee perks? Four questions to ask first," Gallup, August 2017, www.gallup.com/workplace/236141/best-employee-perks-questions-ask-first.aspx.

135 **Millennials are willing to move:** Brigid Schulte, "Millennials want a work life balance. Their bosses just don't get why," *The Washington Post*, May 5, 2015, www.washingtonpost.com/local/millennials-want-a-work-life-balance-their-bosses-just-dont-get-why/2015/05/05/1859369e-f376-11e4-84a6-6d7c67c50db0_story.html.

139 **Buried in their lengthy:** Shauna W., "David Lee Roth explains Van Halen's no brown M&Ms rule," *Ultimate Classic Rock*, 2012, https://ultimateclassicrock.com/david-lee-roth-van-halen-brown-mms-rule.

6: The Neglectful Boss

144 **Failure to communicate:** Eleni Zoe, "Satisfaction with Onboarding: What New Hires Want," TalentLMS, August 22, 2019, www.talentlms.com/blog/new-employee-onboarding-study.

144 **For example, waiting to find out:** C. Lampic et al., "Short- and long-term anxiety and depression in women recalled after breast cancer screening," *European Journal of Cancer* 37, no. 4 (March 2001), https://doi.org/10.1016/S0959-8049(00)00426-3; Patricia Pineault, "Breast Cancer Screening: Women's Experiences of Waiting for Further Testing," *Oncology Nursing Forum* 34, no. 4 (July 2007).

Notes

145 **Experiencing periods of extreme uncertainty**: Kate Sweeny et al., "Two definitions of waiting well," *Emotion* 16, no. 1 (2016), https://doi.org/10.1037/emo0000117.

145 **Burnout is at the highest**: Kristy Threlkeld, "Employee Burnout Report: COVID-19's Impact and 3 Strategies to Curb It," Indeed, March 11, 2021, www.indeed.com/lead/preventing-employee-burnout-report.

145 **particularly high among managers**: Gallup, "The Manager Experience Series: Top Challenges & Perks of Managers," www.gallup.com/workplace/259820/manager-experience-challenges-perk-perspective-paper.aspx?g_source=link_wwwv9&g_campaign=item_259466&g_medium=copy.

145 **One study found that 72 percent**: Alyssa Place, "How managers can protect themselves from burnout," *Employee Benefit News,* March 11, 2021, www.benefitnews.com/news/how-managers-can-protect-themselves-from-burnout.

148 **In large companies**: Randall Beck and James Harter, "Why good managers are so rare," *Harvard Business Review*, March 13, 2014, https://hbr.org/2014/03/why-good-managers-are-so-rare?utm_source=link_wwwv9&utm_campaign=item_231593&utm_medium=copy.

149 **London Business School's**: Julian Birkinshaw and Simon Caulkin, "How Should Managers Spend Their Time? Finding More Time for Real Management," *Business Strategy Review* 23, no. 4 (2012), https://doi.org/10.1111/j.1467-8616.2012.00901.x.

150 **In the modern workplace**: Sharyn E. Herzig and Nerina L. Jimmieson, "Middle managers' uncertainty management during organizational change," *Leadership & Organization Development Journal* 27, no. 8 (2006), https://doi.org/10.1108/01437730610709264.

151 **in short supply is time**: Michael E. Porter and Nitin Nohria, "How CEOs manage time," *Harvard Business Review*, July–August 2018, https://hbr.org/2018/07/the-leaders-calendar#:~:text=The%20leaders%20in%20our%20study,days%2C%20averaging%202.4%20hours%20daily.

153 **About two thirds of people**: Annabel Fenwick Elliott, "Are you a first date fibber? Two thirds of us admit to doing it . . . with men lying most about their wealth and women shaving four years off their age," *Daily Mail*, April 8, 2015, www.dailymail.co.uk/femail/article-3030591/Two-thirds-admit-lying-date.html.

153 **About the same percentage:** HireRight, "Liar, liar! The pants and the rest of you are fired," August 10, 2020, www.hireright.com/blog/tag/lied-on -resume.

154 **The protocol involves:** Philip F. Stahel et al., "The 5th anniversary of the 'Universal Protocol': Pitfalls and pearls revisited," *Patient Safety in Surgery* 3, no. 1 (July 2009), https://doi.org/10.1186/1754-9493-3-14.

154 **In fact, 25 percent:** Balraj S. Jhawar, Demytra Mitsis, and Neil Duggal, "Wrong-sided and wrong-level neurosurgery: A national survey," *Journal of Neurosurgery: Spine SPI* 7, no. 5 (November 2007), https://doi.org/10.3171 /spi-07/11/467.

155 **the Ken Blanchard Companies found:** David Witt, "2020 Leadership development trends, challenges, and opportunities," Ken Blanchard Companies, January 2, 2020, https://resources.kenblanchard.com/blanchard-leaderchat /2020-leadership-development-trends-challenges-and-opportunities.

7: The Gaslighter

171 **There's this mouse:** Ashlee H. Rowe et al., "Voltage-Gated Sodium Channel in Grasshopper Mice Defends Against Bark Scorpion Toxin," *Science* 342, no. 6157 (2013), https://doi.org/10.1126/science.1236451.

172 **Scientists have been studying:** Bella M. DePaulo et al., "Cues to deception," *Psychological Bulletin* 129, no. 1 (2003), https://doi.org/10.1037/0033 -2909.129.1.74.

172 **Individual liars might:** Maria Hartwig and Charles F. Bond, Jr., "Why do lie-catchers fail? A lens model meta-analysis of human lie judgments," *Psychological Bulletin* 137, no. 4 (2011), https://doi.org/10.1037/a0023589.

172 **Most of us hover:** Michael G. Aamodt and Heather Custer, "Who Can Best Catch a Liar?," *Forensic Examiner* 15, no. 1 (Spring 2006); Charles F. Bond and Bella M. DePaulo, "Accuracy of Deception Judgments," *Personality and Social Psychology Review* 10, no. 3 (2006), https://doi.org/10.1207/s15327 957pspr1003_2.

173 **They analyzed nearly thirty thousand:** David F. Larcker and Anastasia A. Zakolyukina, "Detecting Deceptive Discussions in Conference Calls,"

Journal of Accounting Research 50, no. 2 (February 2012), https://doi.org /10.1111/j.1475-679X.2012.00450.x.

174 **Seek out hard evidence**: Hee Sun Park et al., "How people really detect lies," *Communication Monographs* 69, no. 2 (June 2002), https://doi.org/10 .1080/714041710.

175 **Like the leaders**: Bertjan Doosje et al., "Terrorism, radicalization and de-radicalization," *Current Opinion in Psychology* 11 (October 2016), https://doi .org/10.1016/j.copsyc.2016.06.008.

175 **Victims are told that**: Vera E. Mouradian, "Abuse in intimate rela-tionships: Defining the multiple dimensions and terms," National Vio-lence Against Women Research Center, 2000, https://mainweb-v.musc.edu /vawprevention/research/defining.shtml.

176 **Gaslighters are well aware**: David T. Welsh et al., "The slippery slope: How small ethical transgressions pave the way for larger future trans-gressions," *Journal of Applied Psychology* 100, no. 1 (2015), https://doi.org /10.1037/a0036950.

181 **They think, for example**: Todd C. Buckley, Edward B. Blanchard, and W. Trammell Neill, "Information processing and PTSD: A review of the em-pirical literature," *Clinical Psychology Review* 20, no. 8 (November 2000), https://doi.org/10.1016/S0272-7358(99)00030-6; Kate Clauss and Caroline Clements, "Threat Bias and Emotion Recognition in Victims of IPV," *Journal of Interpersonal Violence* 36, nos. 5–6 (March 2018), https://doi.org /10.1177/0886260518766424.

182 **She's found that the best way**: Elizabeth Levy Paluck, Hana Shepherd, and Peter M. Aronow, "Changing climates of conflict: A social network experiment in 56 schools," *Proceedings of the National Academy of Sciences* 113, no. 3 (January 2016), https://doi.org/10.1073/pnas.1514483113.

Quiz 1: Am I a Jerk at Work?

226 **According to a CareerBuilder survey**: Retrieved from www.prnewswire .com/news-releases/more-than-half-of-employers-have-found-content -on-social-media-that-caused-them-not-to-hire-a-candidate-according -to-recent-careerbuilder-survey-300694437.html.

INDEX